The Mysterious Death of Jane Stanford

The Mysterious Death
of Jane Stanford

Robert W. P. Cutler, M.D.

STANFORD GENERAL BOOKS
Stanford University Press
Stanford, California 2003

Stanford University Press
Stanford, California
© 2003 by the Board of Trustees of the
Leland Stanford Junior University
Printed in the United States of America

Library of Congress Cataloging-in-Publication Data

Cutler, Robert W. P.
    The mysterious death of Jane Stanford / Robert W. P. Cutler.
        p.   cm.
    Includes bibliographical references and index.
    ISBN 0-8047-4793-8 (alk. paper)
        1. Stanford, Jane Lathrop, 1828-1905.   2. Murder—Hawaii—
Honolulu—History—Case studies.   3. Poisoning—Hawaii—Honolulu—
History—Case studies.   I. Title.
HV6534.H66 C87   2003
364.15'23'0996931—dc21   2003009915

This book is printed on acid-free, archival quality paper.

Original printing 2003
Last figure below indicates year of this printing:
12   11   10   09   08   07   06   05   04   03

Typeset in 10/13 Sabon

Today there appears to be no good reason for not reporting the known facts.

—Gunther W. Nagel, 1975

Contents

PART III

14 pages of photographs follow page 58

☞ Preface

Had I not stumbled on an account of the episode while researching a book on magnesite mining, I might never have known about the mysterious circumstances of the death of Jane Leland Stanford nearly a century ago. I inquired of several fellow faculty members of the Stanford University School of Medicine, where I have worked for twenty-eight years, and found they shared my ignorance. One friend and colleague, Professor Alberta Siegel, encouraged me to look into the case and pointed me in helpful directions. I regret that Professor Siegel did not live to cast her critical eye on the result. She loved mysteries and was good at figuring how they came out.

I have been exceptionally fortunate in the help I have received—from historians, authors, archivists, librarians, colleagues, and many wonderful friends whom I know only by e-mail—which I gratefully acknowledge here. I wish particularly to thank those at Stanford University who provided source material and answered all my questions: Margaret Kimball, university archivist, and Patricia White and Christy Smith, archives specialists; Roxanne Nilan, past university archivist; Heidi Heilemann of the Lane Medical Library; Esther Wan of the University News Service; Norris Pope, program director of the Stanford University Press; Roger Printup, university registrar; Rene Spicer of the Alumni Association; and Lisa Joo, executive associate in the School of Medicine. My special thanks go to Karen Bartholomew of the Stanford Historical Society, who gave me so much material as well as constructive advice, and to Claude Brinegar, a member of the society. Faculty were equally helpful: W. B. Carnochan generously shared his manuscript on the story of Julius Goebel; James B. D. Mark encouraged me all along; Kenneth Fields put me in touch with Turner Cassity, who kindly gave permission to use his poem "Mrs. Leland Stanford," which germinated when he was a graduate student in the English Department a half-century ago.

I also found library professionals at other institutions wonderfully helpful. Not once did a request go unanswered from Susan Shaner of the Hawaii Judiciary History Center; Duane Fukumoto of the Hawaii State Library; Agnes Conrad, Hawaii state archivist, emerita, and Jolyn Tamura, Hawaii state archivist; Marilyn Reppun of the Hawaiian Mission Children's Society Library; John Weeren of Princeton University; DeeDee Acosta of the University of Hawaii; John Breinich of the Hawaii Medical Library; Stephen Novack of Columbia University; Jeffrey Rosenberg of the Hunterian Society; Paul Banfield of Queen's University, Ontario; and Sigrid Southworth of the Bishop Estate.

Thurston Twigg-Smith of the *Honolulu Advertiser*; Charleen Aina, Hawaii deputy attorney general; Dennis Stillings, the editor of *Healing Islands*; Erica Neves, public relations, Sheraton Moana Surfrider Hotel; Kevin Mullen, retired deputy chief, San Francisco Police Department; and Ronald Englund, Bishop Museum scientist, answered queries that they may have found unusually arcane. Joseph E. Ciotti, professor of physics and astronomy at the University of Hawaii, kindly computed the lunar trajectory over Diamond Head on February 28, 1905.

John Boessenecker (who loaned me his files), Helen Casabona, Gary Ogle, and Stephen Requa (who sent me several chapters of his unpublished book) were most generous in their assistance. My understanding of a main figure in this story could not have developed without the extraordinary help of Marion Follmer, and of Helen Fauss, Ruth Meredith, and Gretchen (Kelbaugh) Wilson, who provided family introductions and shared her lively thoughts. Happenstance allowed me to make the acquaintance, electronically, of Dorothea (Dee) Buckingham, a Honolulu author, ibrarian, and encyclopedic source of information about early twentieth-century Honolulu and Mrs. Stanford's visits. Dee Buckingham is a remarkable friend.

Mrs. Leland Stanford

A plainest Jane. In black brocade and four
Spit curls she is the goddess and machine
To all that she surveys: a brave new world,
Of sandstone courtyards and of red tile roofs.
If it is somehow Sidi-bel-Abbès
In Palo Alto, she is chaperon
Enough to keep the very Legion chaste,
And all Algeria besides. This paint,
However, cannot mock her, nor can we,
For all that earnestness, and let alone
The showing of it, is a true lost art.
Another portrait or another year,
And, like a king in tragedy, who treads
On purple to the axe behind the door,
In summer white, an old executrix
Must go to Honolulu to the cares,
The treacherous companions, and the draught
Of poison on the ship's night-table. You
Who know the guile, the spineless arrogance
Of both the world and the Academy,
How can you doubt that for their paradigms
And for their ease they had their conscience killed?

—Turner Cassity, 1983

☞ Introduction

The Founding of Leland Stanford Junior University

Leland Stanford Jr. was fifteen years old when he died at the Hotel Bristol in Florence, Italy. A physician consulted two weeks earlier had thought his illness typical of typhoid fever and prognosticated full recovery after a period of convalescence. "Leland is nearly at the highest point," Jane Stanford wrote to her close friends Tim and May Hopkins in late February 1884. "The doctor thinks he will be confined for four weeks, even under the most favorable circumstances."[1]

"At the highest point" probably did not refer to a pinnacle of robust recovery, but rather to Leland's fever, which till then had crept up and up, leaving a characteristic sawtooth signature on the temperature graph, to an apex likely in the vicinity of 105°F, a plateau from which the doctor thought it would break and fall. But despite the devoted bedside vigilance of his mother, the tender application of cold wraps by his father, and the fervent prayers of both, the boy succumbed on the morning of March 13, 1884.

Governor Leland Stanford, himself unwell, exhausted, and despondent, lay down to rest. Evidently, while the governor was in a hypnogogic state, he experienced a vision of Leland Jr., who offered guidance that would change his life: "Father, do not say that you have nothing to live for. . . . Live for humanity," or words to that effect.[2] The Stanfords had devoted themselves to the education of their son, had spent years showing him the European centers of history and cultural influence, had encouraged his passion for collecting artifacts, and had engaged tirelessly in his preparation for a life of stimulation and attainment. "Live for humanity," his spirit admonished and Stanford said to his wife, in a truly life-transforming moment: "The children of California shall be my children,"[3] "shall be *our* children," according to an appropriately magnanimous version.[4] The idea of the Leland Stanford Junior University was born.

Leland's death was a tragedy of especially great intensity because he was the only child of older parents—Leland Sr. was sixty, Jane, fifty-five. Their marriage had been barren for nearly eighteen years, and they must have seen Leland's birth as a God-given miracle. It was a time in their lives when extraordinary opulence had replaced the economic uncertainties of the boisterous 1850s. Stanford had been elected governor of California (1862–63) on the Republican ticket. And with the notion of conflict of interest less well defined then than now, he simultaneously occupied the office of president of the Central Pacific Railroad Company (CPRR). Along with Charles Crocker, Mark Hopkins, and Collis Huntington, he was one of the CPRR's "Big Four" (more accurately, the "Big Five," if one includes the legally invaluable Edwin Crocker, Charles's brother, whom Governor Stanford appointed as justice of the California Supreme Court—he resigned after a short term to become counsel for the CPRR).

After forgoing renomination, Stanford put his energies to work as the political and fund-raising figurehead of the CPRR. Hopkins managed the books, Edwin Crocker the legal office, and Charles Crocker the daunting task (dubbed "Nothing Like It in the World" by the historian Stephen E. Ambrose)[5] of railroad construction over and through the Sierra and across the arid, alkaline flats of Nevada to a conjunction with the Union Pacific at Promontory Summit, Utah. Huntington shuttled from New York to Washington as principal lobbyist and was also the chief purchasing agent. Riches came quickly and abundantly, allowing Governor Stanford to enlarge his home in Sacramento, whose forty-four rooms were more than ample, to say the least, for a family of three when Leland Jr. was born on May 14, 1868.

Despite Mrs. Stanford's condition of elderly primigravida (as noted, she was nearly forty), with its attendant risks for both mother and child, there is no record of prenatal difficulty or abnormal labor. One story has it that while she was enjoying a tea party on the verandah, given in anticipation of her confinement, Mrs. Stanford's rocking chair tipped her off the porch and into a bush. She came to no harm; fortunately, her physician was a house guest, and shortly afterwards, he was able to guide her parturition to completion.[6] The incident was said to have put Governor Stanford in a state of shock, however, quite possibly aggravating the pressure he was under from his partners to travel to Salt Lake City and negotiate construction crew contracts with Brigham Young.

A month behind schedule, Stanford finally set off on June 1, 1868, and was gone for about three weeks. On his return to Sacramento, according to legend, Leland asked Jane to organize a dinner for their closest friends so that they might introduce Leland Jr. After the guests were seated, a butler entered carrying a large covered silver platter and placed it at the center of the table. To Mrs. Stanford's astonishment, the governor raised the lid to reveal their infant son supine on a bed of flower petals, and he asked the butler to take the tray with the smiling neonate around to each guest, showing on their left, one presumes, as if serving the entrée.[7] The story is beyond belief, but, like others to be encountered, it has found its way into California history.[8]

Mrs. Stanford and her staff had nearly complete responsibility for nurturing Leland Jr. in his first year of life, because of the frequent business trips to Utah required of his father. On his last and most historic trip, the governor and his party (which curiously did not include any of his partners) set off for Promontory nine days before Leland Jr.'s first birthday to prepare for the golden spike rail line linkage ceremony, scheduled for Saturday, May 8, 1869. In Sacramento that day, Leland Jr. may from his perambulator have witnessed a remarkable celebration of his father's achievement—bands, parades, floats, speeches, and cannon booms—beginning at 5 A.M. and ending "long past what would normally be considered a respectable bedtime."[9] The only thing missing was the prearranged telegram, "OK," signaling that Governor Stanford and Dr. Thomas Durant (on behalf of the Union Pacific Railroad) had driven the last spike.

In fact, there was no signal that day, because when the Stanford party arrived on May 7, Durant's train was not there, and it did not show up until May 10, when the hook-up ceremony was belatedly performed. After the ceremony, Stanford entertained Union Pacific principals in his car, where he is reported to have spoiled the party with a sour grapes remark about government subsidies for the railroad companies being more of a detriment than a benefit. The Union Pacific's workhorse, Dan Casement, felt compelled to raise his champagne glass: "Mr. President of the Central Pacific: If this subsidy has been such a detriment to the building of these roads, I move you, sir, that it be returned to the United States Government with our compliment."[10]

Casement's rejoinder was remarkable. It portended precisely the government's point of view when it filed suit against the governor's estate more than fifteen years later, placing Jane Stanford in a position she could never have imagined for herself.[11]

Leland Jr. developed into an exceptionally intelligent and inquisitive lad. He started to collect artifacts so seriously and in such quantity that his parents planned to erect a private museum for his collections, first in San Francisco, later on the university campus. By then, the Stanfords had moved from Sacramento to San Francisco, where they built another mansion on Nob Hill. They took the boy to visit European cities, archaeological sites, and fashionable resorts. On her first trip abroad with Leland Jr. in 1880, Mrs. Stanford (the governor would join them in 1881) made the acquaintance of Andrew D. White, president of Cornell University, at the Hôtel des Anglais at Nice. In his letter of condolences after Leland's death, White remembered the "dear and noble boy . . . especially being struck by his manliness and his simple, substantial, thoughtful character which was already definitely formed in him."[12] Leland was but twelve years old.

Neither Governor nor Mrs. Stanford ever wavered from their goal of building a university. With the design concepts of Frederick Law Olmsted, architectural plans of Shepley, Rutan and Coolidge, and close guidance of General Francis A. Walker, president of the Massachusetts Institute of Technology, Leland and Jane set the cornerstone on their Palo Alto Stock Farm on May 14, 1887. It was the nineteenth anniversary of Leland Jr.'s birth. Design changes, and the prolonged absences of the Stanfords in Washington, D.C. (Leland had been elected senator in 1885), delayed construction, and it was not until spring 1891 that it looked certain that the university would start enrolling students in the fall. Senator and Mrs. Stanford left Washington in their private railroad car to find a president, a man whom the senator would select based on his scholarship and business sense.

"If I cannot combine these two qualifications," the senator had told a newsman, " I will take the presidency myself until I can get a suitable man."[13] Their quest ended on a siding in Bloomington, Indiana, after Cornell's Andrew White turned down the offer and recommended his former student David Starr Jordan, then president of the University of Indiana. After brief meetings, Leland with President Jordan, possibly Jane with Mrs. Jordan, and the Jordans with each other, the job was offered and accepted on the spot. Jordan would later say his main worry was one of the terms of the Founding Grant: "the new institution was to be 'personally conducted,' its sole trustee a business man who was, moreover, active in political life."[14]

In fact, after Senator Stanford died two years later, the "sole trustee" became Jane Stanford. Although a 24-member Board of Trustees had been appointed when the Founding Grant had been signed in 1885, the charter had "reserv[ed] to the grantors, during their lives, . . . the right to exercise all the functions, powers, and duties of the Trustees."[15] The board did not meet formally until 1897 and did not assume responsibility for oversight of the university until 1903, when Mrs. Stanford relinquished control, only to be elected president of the board.

Some (perhaps many) saw her as an unyielding autocrat. Speaking admiringly of Jordan, one graduate reminisced, "The marvel is that he was able to keep the peace (most of the time) between Mrs. Stanford, with her dictatorial powers and her emotional nature, and his young bronco faculty."[16] Others saw her as the mother of the "children of California." A Stanford student, Carolus Ager (Charles Kellogg Field's pen name), put it best:

> We reverence his memory,—
> The power of his name
> Is in our loyal hearts to-day,
> The impulse of his fame;
> But ah, how can her children's love
> Be adequately shown
> The mother-heart that folded us
> And fought for us alone!
>
> Gray mother of our fostered youth . . .[17]

And with extraordinary courage, devotion, and spirit, Mrs. Stanford labored to the time of her death on the objective she and Leland had set for themselves the night Leland Jr. died. As President Jordan wrote: "Jefferson was in the seventies when he turned back to his early ambition, the foundation of the University of Virginia. The mother of Stanford University was older than Jefferson before she laid down the great work of her life as completed."[18]

"I wish . . . to tell the story of a noble life, of one of the bravest, wisest, most patient, most courageous and most devout of all the women who have ever lived," David Starr Jordan began when he addressed the gathering that celebrated Founders' Day on March 9, 1909. The annual celebration included the laying of a wreath at the mausoleum in which Leland and Jane Stanford were interred with Leland Jr. Perhaps some in the crowd of students and parents knew that it would have been Senator Leland Stanford's eighty-fifth birthday. Probably few were aware, as was President Jordan, that on the same day four years earlier, a coroner's jury had concluded that Jane Lathrop Stanford, the subject of Jordan's tribute, had been murdered.[19]

PART ONE

1 ⁓ The Death of Mrs. Stanford

Picnic at the Pali

The weather was mild in Honolulu the day Jane Stanford died, her personal secretary Bertha Berner recalls in her memoir. Mrs. Stanford had thoroughly enjoyed a picnic lunch, sitting comfortably on carriage cushions set down in a grove of trees overlooking the ocean on the far side of the Pali. The only aggravation in an otherwise splendid day had been the delay in leaving the Moana Hotel at the scheduled hour of 10 A.M. The gingerbread had failed to rise, and Mrs. Stanford was displeased to have to wait while a new loaf was prepared in the kitchen. Once the party was under way, however, her irritation dispensed with, she sang in the back seat of the surrey and chattered with keen anticipation about further travels in Hawaii and then Japan. In her memoir, which was published thirty years later, Berner remembers her concern over Mrs. Stanford's indulgence in chocolates and undercooked gingerbread at the picnic lunch: "I really was uneasy, for as a rule she ate very carefully, scarcely ever much that was sweet, as the doctor had forbidden it."[1]

Whether Berner's memoir was based on a diary or was simply embellished is not known. She describes the day in fine detail. She read to Mrs. Stanford from Marie Corelli's *The Mighty Atom*, purchased that morning at the hotel newsstand. The popular novel—about an English couple's only child, Lionel, who believes he has no soul—saddened Miss Berner. (She may have stumbled reading aloud the accented prattle of three-year-old Jasmine, who befriends Lionel: "Would 'ee like an apple? I'll gi' ye this, if s'be ye'se let me bite th' red bit oot").[2]

Following the reading, at about three o'clock, the party started for the hotel at Waikiki, gladdened by Mrs. Stanford's cheerful spirits. She rested before dinner. Having eaten too heartily at the picnic lunch, she dined simply on a plate of hot soup and requested a cup of Garfield tea, a remedy for constipation and sick headache then in vogue. After supper, she and Miss Berner strolled to the pavilion at the end of the pier. There they encountered Mrs. Stanford's new maid, May Hunt, and Mrs. Stanford asked May to carry their parasols back to the hotel. Mrs. Stanford and Miss Berner stayed to watch the moon rise, "a glorious sight that evening," according to Berner's memoir.

The actual facts as given by Berner while under oath thirty years earlier, on March 6, 1905, not only lacked the literary adornments of her memoir but also, more important, differed in detail.

For example, Berner said in sworn testimony that the party had a "carriage order at 10 A.M. [and] we got off on time."[3] May Hunt agreed. Neither mentioned an irritating delay caused by failure of gingerbread to rise. The *Honolulu Pacific Commercial Advertiser*, covering the case, reported that the Moana picnic basket had contained meat and cheese sandwiches, boiled eggs, and a fresh loaf of gingerbread.[4] Berner told reporters that they enjoyed the standard cold dishes prepared by the hotel. The contents of Mrs. Stanford's picnic lunch would seem too inconsequential to dwell upon were it not that the "surfeit of unsuitable food" factored into the cause of death later advanced by Dr. Jordan.[5]

Unsettled as well is the question of the weather encountered by the picnicking group. The temperature reached 77°F in Honolulu that day. It was pleasantly mild, and the temperature had "not turned perceptibly chillier" as the afternoon wore on, Berner remembered in 1935— whereas in 1905, she had written to Dr. Ernest C. Waterhouse saying that Mrs. Stanford had sat in the shade of a tree "fully an hour in a very strong and rather chilly wind."[6] Dr. Waterhouse, who was commissioned to review the inquest and autopsy reports of Mrs. Stanford's death, thus found that Mrs. Stanford had sat "in the cold wind for an hour . . . the undue exposure at this time . . . [placing] an unusual strain on her that day"? [7] It had been an "unusual exposure," Jordan summed up in his press release fifteen days after Mrs. Stanford's death.[8]

Furthermore, at the inquest, Miss Berner testified that following a light supper of soup, she and Mrs. Stanford had sat on the veranda, where Mrs. Stanford chatted with Mrs. W. C. Peacock. (Mr. Peacock, the owner of the Moana Hotel, would shortly be called upon to serve

on a coroner's jury and view Mrs. Stanford's corpse.) At around eight
P.M., on the way to her room, Mrs. Stanford admitted having eaten too
much candy and requested "a little medicine," but specifically *declined*
an offer of Garfield tea. She did not walk to the pier pavilion, and she
did not ask Miss Hunt to return her parasol to her room. The parasol
exchange had actually occurred two days earlier, and it caused quite a
stir in the Honolulu police office because of the suspicions of Mr.
W. H. Nelson.

Bertha Berner and Jane Stanford had not even watched the glorious
moonrise, as Berner claimed. The moon was a waning crescent on February 28, 1905, and it rose at 2:53 A.M.

Calling attention to these minute details of Mrs. Stanford's last day
is not intended to disparage Miss Berner, whose memoir chronicles
many interesting facets of her employer's life. It is the story of Mrs.
Stanford's *death* that is problematic, for two reasons: (1) it is replete
with inaccuracies; and (2) the inaccuracies have been represented as
facts in many historical accounts that derive from Berner's writings.
Actually, Berner's version is so slanted that it neither informs her readers that Mrs. Stanford had taken a dose of bicarbonate of soda containing strychnine a short while before her death nor tells them that a
coroner's jury determined that she had been murdered. Berner's sworn
testimony at the coroner's inquest, her memory fresh and unaffected by
subsequent persuasions, is more likely to be a correct representation of
the events of February 28. Fortunately, the coroner's records have been
preserved.

Moana Hotel, February 28, 1905

When preparing to retire at about 8:30 that evening, Mrs. Stanford
asked Miss Berner to put out her medications on the dressing table,
medications that she often used as digestive aids. Berner testified that
she had scooped half a teaspoon of bicarbonate of soda from a small,
wide-mouthed bottle (Hunt testified "a teaspoon") and placed the
spoon on the nightstand, together with a cascara capsule. It is important to know that this was the first time Mrs. Stanford had requested
bicarbonate of soda since she and her companions had left San Francisco two weeks earlier. At 9 o'clock, Berner and Hunt retired to the
room they shared across from No. 120, Mrs. Stanford's room. Hunt

testified she shortly returned to No. 120 to show Mrs. Stanford how to lock the door. Hunt then fell asleep, only to be awakened by sounds from an adjacent room that she took to be those of a guest vomiting.

She dozed again until approximately 11:15 P.M., when she heard Mrs. Stanford call "May" in a distressed voice. Berner was also awakened by Mrs. Stanford's cry—"Bertha, May, I am so sick." They rushed to her room, as did Mr. Adam Heunisch, a guest in the room next to Mrs. Stanford's. The *Pacific Commercial Advertiser* and the *San Francisco Chronicle* reported that Heunisch had heard a commotion and, upon entering her room, had found Mrs. Stanford writhing on the floor in agony, moaning as if in pain. Other newspapers quoted Heunisch as having found Mrs. Stanford standing at her door.

Berner testified that Heunisch appeared at about the time she reached Mrs. Stanford, who was standing in her open doorway, clutching the frame. This version seems more credible, in that Mrs. Stanford's locked door would have barred Heunisch's entry. Had he somehow gained access, however, and found Mrs. Stanford prostrate on the floor, his testimony might have answered a subsequent question as to how Mrs. Stanford could possibly have arisen without assistance had she been thrown out of bed to the floor. Curiously, Heunisch appears not to have testified at the inquest, despite his having been subpoenaed as a witness.[9]

What happened during the next twenty minutes was described by Miss Berner, Miss Hunt, Dr. Francis Howard Humphris, and Dr. Harry Vicars Murray in clear, concise and concordant testimony. Mrs. Stanford cried out to her companions, "Bertha, run for the doctor. I have no control of my body. I think I have been poisoned again." Berner rushed to the elevator and told the attendant urgently to fetch Dr. Humphris, who had rooms upstairs, and whom she had met casually the previous week, and perhaps even years earlier. At the same time, Heunisch ran to the stairwell, also, it seems likely, to summon Humphris. The doctor was already up. He had been aroused from sleep by the commotion of commands from the lower floor: first to fetch a doctor, then to send for Doctor Humphris. As he was pulling up his trousers and stepping into his boots, someone knocked on his door— whether the elevator boy or Mr. Heunisch he did not know.

Dr. Humphris hurried to Mrs. Stanford's room, where he found her standing by the washstand, supported by Miss Berner and Miss Hunt, trying to sip water. Drinking the warm water offered by her secretary was difficult for Mrs. Stanford; she complained, "I cannot take it, my jaws are set." A moment earlier, after Berner had rubbed her cheeks and urged her with anxiety in her voice to drink, Mrs. Stanford had managed to swallow several glasses of warm water, at which point Dr. Humphris had arrived. Unfortunately, the water did not induce vomiting. Even a subsequent glassful of mustard water, prepared and administered by Humphris after he removed Mrs. Stanford's dentures, brought up only an ounce of gastric contents.

More vomiting might have been induced had there been more time. As Humphris tried to administer a solution of bromine and chloral hydrate, Mrs. Stanford, now in anguish, exclaimed, "My jaws are stiff [Humphris confirmed the contraction of her jaw muscles by palpation]. This is a horrible death to die." Whereupon she was seized by a tetanic spasm that progressed relentlessly to a state of severe rigidity: her jaws clamped shut, her thighs opened widely, her feet twisted inwards, her fingers and thumbs clenched into tight fists, and her head drew back. Finally, her respiration ceased. Dr. Humphris estimated that the spasm lasted three minutes.

In the few moments before death, Mrs. Stanford was alert and rational. She told Humphris that she had been thrown out of bed by a spasm. She said she had no pain. She had arisen to take the bicarbonate of soda and a cascara capsule sometime after Berner and Hunt had left. She thought she had been poisoned and said that she had been poisoned before. She asked Humphris to bring a stomach pump and instructed Berner to inform him about the incident in San Francisco. On learning that Mrs. Stanford had some weeks earlier been the near-victim of strychnine poisoning, Humphris pocketed the bottles of bicarbonate of soda and cascara tablets, but not before tasting a minute sample of the soda. It tasted bitter, he said, "a bitterness that I associated with nux vomica or strychnia."

With this medical history, Dr. Humphris acted quickly. He hurried to his rooms to obtain the mustard emetic; he went to the lobby to telephone Dr. Francis Root Day to bring a stomach pump with utmost haste for a case of suspected strychnine poisoning; he sent a concerned guest (presumably Mr. Heunisch) to his rooms to fetch his medical bags; and when Mrs. Stanford began her fatal spasm, he sent the guest to find Dr. Murray.

Dr. Day counted many of the city's prominent families among his patients, and it would not be surprising if some had sent their sons and daughters to Stanford University. Whether this thought flashed through Humphris's mind or his professional esteem alone dictated Dr. Day's selection is unknown. Murray's recruitment was straightforward; he resided at the Moana Hotel and was known to be "in house" at that hour.

When Dr. Murray arrived, he found Mrs. Stanford sitting erect in a chair, supported on either side by Humphris and Hunt, with her head extended, her eyes bulging, and her pupils dilated. On taking her wrist and feeling her brow, Murray noticed that Mrs. Stanford's temperature was elevated. She was not breathing, although Humphris thought he detected a flicker of a pulse. Murray testified how he was struck by the intensity of the spasm that appeared to be still in progress. Her thumbs were tightly clenched in her fists, her knees were spread widely apart, and her feet were turned up with a markedly exaggerated arch. The two physicians exchanged glances and carried Mrs. Stanford to the bed, at which point her jaw relaxed and dropped open. She was dead.

During this dramatic illness, which ran its course in no more than fifteen or twenty minutes, Berner and Hunt had done their best to reassure Mrs. Stanford and make her comfortable. They sent to the kitchen for hot water in which to bathe Mrs. Stanford's hands and feet. They massaged her limbs and cheeks with alcohol. ("The two girls," Dr. Jordan wrote later, "were busy with treatment which would have produced instant death in strychnine poisoning.")[10] For a few moments, her condition appeared to improve; she was comfortable, and Berner thought she looked better. She reassured Mrs. Stanford that she was "coming out alright." At which point, Mrs. Stanford cried out that another spasm was beginning. Surely knowing she was about to die, she implored, "Oh God, forgive me my sins . . . is my soul prepared to meet my dear ones?" Those were the words Miss Berner recalled at the inquest on March 6, 1905.

Dr. Day arrived five minutes after Mrs. Stanford died, at about 11:45 P.M. He brought the stomach pump, a bottle of chloroform for anesthesia, and a preparation of chloral hydrate and tannic acid, used as an antidote to strychnine. Humphris informed him in the hotel lobby of Mrs. Stanford's demise and escorted him to her room. When Day looked at Mrs. Stanford's body lying on the bed, one aspect struck him. He later told the coroner's jury that he had been "impressed with one conspicuous feature, and that was the rigidity . . . the position of the feet; the ankle was in extreme extension, that is, the toes thrown down

so that the arch of the foot was very much exaggerated and drawn in-
ward toward the middle line, a condition that I don't recall having seen
before on any body."

Securing the Evidence

The five persons (six if Mr. Heunisch were still present) who gathered
at the bedside were stunned. All three physicians knew the case would
become celebrated and be the subject of a forensic investigation, in
which they would play leading roles. Leaving Berner and Hunt to deal
privately with their emotions, Humphris and Murray gathered the material evidence. Humphris had already pocketed the bottles of bicarbonate of soda and cascara capsules, and he picked up the empty glass
and spoon on the bedside stand. Murray carried the chamber pot into
which Mrs. Stanford had vomited an ounce of gastric contents. All
three physicians retired to Humphris's sitting room, where Day and
Murray remained in possession of the evidence while Humphris took a
carriage to the Honolulu cable office. Before Humphris departed, Day
and Murray also tasted the bicarbonate of soda; each agreed that it had
a bitterness characteristic of strychnia or nux vomica, as Day later explained to the coroner's jury, "a bitter taste which certainly was foreign
to the taste of pure bicarbonate."

Dr. Humphris, presumably acting on instructions from Miss Berner,
sent cables to the mainland, one to Mrs. Stanford's brother, Charles G.
Lathrop, and the other to her attorney, Mountford S. Wilson. The cables were the same and conveyed the essential information: "Mrs. Stanford died suddenly."[11] Humphris then drove to the police station, from
which he telephoned Deputy Sheriff William T. Rawlins over the
Gamewell line, a private phone line from headquarters to the deputy
sheriff's house. Humphris informed Rawlins of his suspicion that Mrs.
Stanford had died of strychnine poisoning. The doctor then picked up
Judge William L. Stanley at his home (he was not a guest at the Moana
Hotel, as told in some accounts), and they drove out to the hotel.

Deputy Sheriff Rawlins was waiting for Dr. Humphris and Judge
Stanley in the lobby. Together they proceeded to room 120 to view
Mrs. Stanford's body (Miss Berner and Miss Hunt were still there) and
then continued on to Humphris's apartment, where the other physicians waited. The medicine bottles and other articles were handed over
to the sheriff, who wrapped the chamber pot, glass, and spoon in paper

and put the bottles in his pocket. At 5 A.M., still in the company of
Judge Stanley, Rawlins conveyed all of these items to Dr. John S. B.
Pratt, the chief sanitary officer of the Hawaii Territorial Board of
Health, who had also been summoned to Mrs. Stanford's room. Pratt
pocketed the medicine bottles, wedged the wrapped items between his
feet on the floor of his buggy, and drove back to town.

Deputy Sheriff Rawlins had a busy night. By law, he served as the
coroner. Before Mrs. Stanford's body could be removed, territorial pe-
nal law required a viewing by a coroner's jury. Rawlins called upon
Mr. Peacock, who assisted in gathering together six jurors—Mr. Peacock, himself, and his manager, J. H. Hertsche; three guests of the hotel, T. A. Hays, H. Jeffrey, and W. J. Harvey; and a nearby resident,
E. S. Cunha. The viewing took place in the private dining room of the
Moana Hotel at 4 A.M. on March 1, 1905. Shortly thereafter, the undertaker, Henry Williams, took Mrs. Stanford's body to the Queen's
Hospital morgue. These same jurors would sit through three days of
hearings the following week (failure to appear could result in a fine of
up to $5).

The Autopsy

The autopsy on Mrs. Stanford was conducted in the morgue of Queen's
Hospital by Dr. Clifford Brown Wood, who served as pathologist at
the request of Dr. Humphris. Because he, Murray, and Day had been
closely involved in Mrs. Stanford's crisis, Humphris thought that it
would be prudent to call upon Wood, whose professional opinion
would not be influenced by personal engagement in her terminal illness. Dr. Wood was the senior house surgeon at Queen's Hospital, a
position he had held for more than ten years. He had a great deal of
experience conducting postmortem examinations. Given the possibility
of murder, the propriety of Humphris's selection is hard to argue, although it served later to add Dr. Wood to Dr. Jordan's list of conspira-
tors. Curiously, aside from newspaper reports, historical accounts of
Mrs. Stanford's autopsy have not identified Wood as the pathologist,
or prosector, as the conductor of an autopsy is called.

The autopsy began at 9 A.M. on March 1. Those present, in addition
to the morgue assistant and the mortician Williams, included Robert
Duncan, a chemist, and seven physicians—Drs. Wood, Humphris,
Murray, Day, and Pratt, as well as two interested observers, Frank E.

Sawyer and William E. Taylor. All seven physicians were highly respected members of the Honolulu medical community. Dr. Taylor,
who only attended part of the autopsy, was the senior physician present, aged sixty-seven. He had been a naval surgeon during the Civil
War and later, for twenty years, professor of surgery at the University
of California; Humphris invited him to attend the postmortem as a
professional courtesy. Dr. Sawyer, aged thirty, was the youngest. He
was a recent graduate of the Cooper Medical College, where he would
have been taught pathology by Dr. William Ophüls, the physician who
is usually cited as the final authority on the cause of Mrs. Stanford's
death.

Robert Duncan attended the autopsy as toxicologist. He held a
Bachelor of Science degree in chemistry from the University of California and had recently been appointed as food commissioner for the Territory of Hawaii, succeeding Dr. Edmund Shorey. Duncan had an adequate laboratory at the Free Dispensary building in Honolulu, where,
at the time, he was engaged in quantifying the basic nutritional elements of native algae in collaboration with Miss Minnie Reed, a science teacher at the Kamehameha Schools, who was investigating the
economic value of seaweed. Although expert in such basic chemistry,
Duncan's skill as a forensic scientist is uncertain. He had received the
medicines and other objects from Dr. Pratt earlier that morning and
now awaited samples from Mrs. Stanford's autopsy.

As Dr. Wood performed the necropsy, describing his findings as he
went along in the customary manner, Dr. Day took notes. The transcribed report was at slight variance with autopsy reporting practice, in
that some sections used the past tense instead of the traditional present
tense.[17] In other respects, the report followed standard protocol, at the
outset describing the general external characteristics of the body, such
as size, nourishment, hair, teeth, skin, and posture and muscle tone of
the limbs. Dr. Waterhouse later characterized it as a "meager report,"
but it was made slim by its cryptic notations, not by its lack of information, as Waterhouse implied.

A key point of the external examination was the absence of a cuta-
neous or mucous membrane wound, sought carefully by Dr. Wood to
rule out tetanus infection, or lockjaw, in which the spasm is indistin-
guishable from that suffered by Mrs. Stanford.[18] The rigidity of the
muscles—the jaws, forearms, hands, thighs, legs, and feet—impressed
Wood and the others. It was far greater than normal rigor mortis.

When he straightened out the fingers, they immediately recoiled into a fist. Wood commented, with some thoroughness, that, oddly, the muscles of the arms were relaxed, unlike all of the others. He later learned why: Mr. Williams, with considerable effort, had had to forcibly reduce the abnormal rigor in order to ungown the body.

The fixity of the terminal posture of Mrs. Stanford's feet was striking to Dr. Wood, who dictated: "[F]eet adducted and flaxed [sic], exaggerating the arch of the foot in a marked degree. Toes in state of extension, especially the great toe. This existed in both feet, but more especially in the right foot."[14] Later at the inquest, Wood, Humphris, Day, and Murray commented on the pedal posture, which the physician-artist Sir Charles Bell had dramatically illustrated in a drawing of a soldier in the throes of a tetanus spasm.[15] The physical sign was as specific as any could be in medicine. Each physician was convinced of its diagnostic meaning. It was, perhaps, the unwavering unity of professional opinion that spawned President Jordan's subsequent charge of conspiracy.

Following an incision from sternal notch to pubis, Wood turned his attention to the abdominal cavity and organs. He found nothing of note—injection of superficial blood vessels on the serosal surface of the stomach, an absence of gastric distension, the expected senile changes of the pelvic organs, several gallstones, yet patency of the biliary ducts—that would point to one diagnosis or another. The thorax, heart, and lungs were examined next. The lungs had a dusky color. The heart, about the state of which much would subsequently be made, was not enlarged. Scattered whitish plaques were noted in the myocardium. Both auricles contained dark, liquid blood.[16] The right ventricle was flabby and empty; the left contracted with a small quantity of dark blood in its chamber. Wood described fatty changes in the wall of the right ventricle, as well as what he considered insignificant atheromatous plaques of the mitral and semilunar valves and of the aorta. "All the valves of the heart and vessels competent," Dr. Wood concluded.

The final step in the autopsy consisted in removal of the brain for fixation by Dr. Day. The external appearance did not elicit comment from Wood except to note the nonspecific, yet marked, injection of the meningeal membranes. Because of its soft consistency, it was customary to examine the interior of the brain after hardening in fixatives. Wood also gave the heart to Day for preservation, and he turned over to Mr. Duncan the liver, kidneys, stomach, large and small intestines, two ounces of urine, and, in separate bottles, the liquid contents of the stomach and intestines. The medical examination of Mrs. Stanford in Honolulu concluded at noon. For Dr. Humphris, it had lasted more than twelve hours. For Mr. Duncan, the day was just beginning.

2 ⌒ The Poland Water Poisoning

Nob Hill, January 14, 1905

Early on the morning of March 1, 1905, the *Daily Palo Alto*, the Stanford University student newspaper, ran a special issue headlining Dr. Humphris's telegram to Mr. Lathrop, Mrs. Stanford's brother and the business manager of the university. "Mrs. Stanford Dies Suddenly in Hawaii," the extra reported, adding, "according to the best information obtainable, her death was due to terminal pneumonia." When the regular issue appeared later in the day, the *Daily* had somewhat more accurate information to report, including the suspicion of strychnine poisoning and the nagging respiratory infection that the editors learned had taken Mrs. Stanford to Hawaii in the first place. The column ended with the news that "a few days before contracting the fatal cold, Mrs. Stanford drank some mineral water which is reported to have contained some foreign substance. This nauseated her, but is believed to have left no permanent effect."[1]

That was the very occasion about which Mrs. Stanford had asked Miss Berner to inform Dr. Humphris, as she struggled with the certain awareness that she was dying of strychnine poisoning. Although the earlier episode of exposure to strychnine had taken place on Saturday, January 14, 1905, the story was not disclosed to the public until February 18, 1905, when it was released to the *San Francisco Chronicle*. By then, Mrs. Stanford was steaming to Honolulu on the SS *Korea*. The only witnesses to this occurrence at the Nob Hill mansion were Bertha Berner and Elizabeth Richmond, Mrs. Stanford's personal maid. Berner later told the story to Dr. Humphris, the Honolulu coroner's jury, the newspapers, and officials of Stanford University. She would recount the event in her memoir. Richmond gave several newspaper interviews, and her concise signed statement was published in Fremont Older's *San Francisco Bulletin*.[2]

The daytime events of January 14, 1905, are not known with certainty. In her memoir, Berner writes that Mrs. Stanford met with her attorney, Russell Wilson, in the morning and conducted a Stanford Board of Trustees meeting in the afternoon. The fatigue resulting from these activities prompted her to retire early. Mrs. Stanford's close friend, confidant, and advisor, Judge George E. Crothers, a member of Stanford's pioneer class, recalled things differently when he wrote to Mrs. Fremont Older more than forty years later, prefacing his remarks by saying, "I would hope that it [his memory] might be a little better . . . than that of Miss Berner."[3]

Crothers pointed out correctly that Russell Wilson had suffered a paralytic stroke several years earlier, said that the Board of Trustees (of which he was a member) had met on Fridays, and thought that he had attended a dinner given by Mrs. Stanford in honor of her niece, Jennie Stanford Lathrop, on the evening of January 14. Newspaper reports indicate, however, that the reception for Miss Lathrop had been scheduled for February 8 and had been cancelled. Mrs. Stanford, about to embark on the *Korea*, wrote a last letter to her friend May Hopkins, regretting that she had needed "to recall the 'at home' for dear Jennie."[4] But perhaps Mrs. Stanford held more than one dinner party for Miss Lathrop.

Whichever account or combination thereof is correct has no obvious bearing on what happened that night, except that each version places a large number of people—trustees in the one case, dinner guests in the other—at the Stanford mansion on January 14. Either rendition lengthens the list of persons who could have visited the supply of Poland Mineral Spring Water, stored in the houseboy's pantry, and spiked a bottle with strychnine.[5]

Berner and Richmond are in generally close agreement about what happened. It was around 9 P.M. (suggesting that no dinner party was given that evening) when Richmond, who was sitting in the sewing room next to Mrs. Stanford's bedroom, was summoned to taste the Poland water, of which Mrs. Stanford had just drunk a glassful. Richmond remarked on its bitterness, and, despite finding that her mistress had already induced vomiting by inserting her fingers into her pharynx, Richmond persuaded Mrs. Stanford to drink four or five glasses of warm water, all of which she "threw off" promptly. Richmond then fetched Berner from her room upstairs; the secretary added her opinion that the water had a "queer taste." After noting flocculent material in the water, the three women agreed that a chemical analysis should be undertaken. Richmond said she took the bottle that night to the Wakelee Drug Store at the corner of Montgomery and Bush Streets (a night watchman corroborated her story). Berner says it was the next morning.

A few hours one way or the other, although this would later be an element in an unusual theory developed by private detectives, did not affect the timeliness of the analysis, because Wakelee's had to send the bottle of contaminated water to the Falkenau Assaying Company on Sacramento Street. Louis Falkenau, the chemist, did not issue a preliminary report until the following Saturday, January 21, and a final report until January 31, 1905. His preliminary qualitative analysis disclosed the presence of strychnine in the Poland water; the final quantitative report detailed the type and quantity of the poison. There were traces of brucine and other impurities, suggesting that it was a "common article of commerce"—that is, rodent poison.[6] A water-glass-full contained 0.8 grains, an amount in excess of the dose, Falkenau pointed out with professional thoroughness, "that proved fatal in the case of Dr. Warren in 14 minutes."[7]

Elizabeth Richmond may well have deserved credit for saving Mrs. Stanford's life. Instead, she was dismissed from the household (she had planned to leave anyway), hounded by detectives, shadowed and grilled relentlessly, and many years later named by Dr. Jordan as the poisoner of the Poland water.

The Harry Morse Detective and Patrol Agency

On the urging of her physician, Dr. William Boericke (who was first consulted on January 21), and others close to her, Mrs. Stanford (and Miss Berner) left the Nob Hill mansion to seek seclusion and rest at the Hotel Vendome, a resort in San Jose, two days after receiving the first report from Mr. Falkenau.[8] She suffered not only from a nagging respiratory infection but also from the horrifying realization that someone had tried to kill her. She was ill and depressed, and the cold and constant rain did little to ease either condition. A decision was made to go to a warmer climate, and plans were laid to travel to Hawaii, and then on to Japan if her condition permitted. Accordingly, she and Berner returned by train to San Francisco, where they were met by Mountford Wilson and Charles Lathrop, as Berner remembers in her memoir, making no mention of a stop in Palo Alto to purchase sundries and bicarbonate of soda. The men escorted them to the St. Francis Hotel, where they lodged until departing for Honolulu on February 14, 1905.

These same advisors had conferred with Mrs. Stanford the day she first learned that the Poland water contained poison. They decided that an investigation was wanted, a private and discrete study, not a police investigation. Wilson retained the Harry Morse Detective and Patrol Agency, a private detective firm founded in 1878. Mr. Morse was nearly seventy years old, but he retained much of the dash and flair of his younger days as sheriff of Alameda County, from which office he had been involved in legendary feats of derring-do.[9] He had silenced the notorious bandits Narato Ponce and Juan Soto and had ridden for two months in tireless pursuit of the murderer Tiburcio Vasquez (although he failed to catch him). His skill as a detective had put the stage robber Black Bart in San Quentin. Ned Buntline fictionalized him in the dime novel *Red Dick, the Tiger of California*. Except for bad press when he had assisted the defense at the murder trial of the Cooper Medical College student William Henry Theodore Durrant, the so-called "demon in the belfry,"[10] Morse was generally thought of as the finest detective in San Francisco. He was discrete and self-assured.

Morse assigned his lead detective, Jules Callundan, to conduct the investigation. Callundan had been with the Morse agency since his teenage years and had risen to the rank of captain. He, too, was discrete. His sleuthing went completely unnoticed by the press until the *San Francisco Chronicle* disclosed it on February 18. Neither Callundan's investigative strategy nor his findings have been preserved except in newspaper accounts, as is the case with the details of most San Francisco murders committed around the time of the 1906 earthquake. Nonetheless, the basic facts can be gleaned and sifted from the hyperbole and sensationalism that characterized news reporting in 1905.

Callundan immediately assigned a gumshoe to tail Elizabeth Richmond. The maid remained at the Stanford mansion until January 26, when she was released and given severance pay by one of Charles Lathrop's clerks. Richmond always insisted that her departure from Mrs. Stanford's household had been planned months before and awaited only the hiring of a new maid (May Hunt). Richmond left that evening in the company of Nora Hopkins, a housemaid at the campus

home, and took a room in a friend's boarding house at 111 Sutter
Street. She suspected at once that she was being tailed. Her suspicion
was confirmed the following day when she spotted the stranger she had
seen the night before huddled behind a newspaper at the Third and
Townsend train depot while on her way to Palo Alto to retrieve her
belongings. Richmond was upset but hardly surprised to find herself
under surveillance. She suspected that she had fallen under suspicion
when Mrs. Stanford assigned her duties and bedroom to Nora Hopkins; to her credit, she grew to accept the suspicion as understandable.

Alone and frightened, Richmond sent a note to Alfred Beverly, Mrs.
Stanford's former butler (he had earlier been the butler of the famous
English actress Lillie Langtry, he boasted), who had left her employment many months earlier and resided in San Mateo. Beverly was English, like Richmond, and he had, in fact, recommended her as a personal maid to Mrs. Stanford, whom they had both accompanied on her
worldwide travels in 1903–4, along with Berner. Richmond remembered that she had been employed around the time Reverend Heber
Newton had resigned as pastor of the Memorial Church at Stanford, in
May 1903. Newton's tenure had been a disappointment to Mrs. Stanford, and she may well have discussed it with her new maid.

Beverly was irate at the treatment Richmond received at the hands
of the Morse agents. She had been under surveillance for nearly two
weeks when, on Saturday, February 11, two detectives appeared at the
Sutter Street boarding house to interrogate her. That Monday, Jules
Callundan and Mountford Wilson questioned her for a second time.
Richmond gave them a full account of the events of January 14. Normally, the houseboy, Ah Young, took a fresh bottle of Poland water to
Mrs. Stanford's bedroom each day, but on January 13, he had forgotten to do so. As a result, Richmond remembered, she had asked the
butler to uncork a bottle and had placed it on Mrs. Stanford's washstand herself. The next morning, Richmond noted that some of the water had been drunk, but she did not replenish it. Seemingly satisfied
with her responses, Callundan took her address (she was going to San
Mateo to stay at the Beverlys'), and he did not contact her again until
after Mrs. Stanford's death. When Richmond told Beverly about the
ordeal of her interrogation, he reported the affair to the British consul.

The Morse agency combed through druggists' records in San Francisco, San Jose, and Palo Alto for strychnine sales to a member of the
Stanford household but found none. Callundan interviewed the other

servants, and although he learned that petty jealousies existed, largely focused on Bertha Berner, he did not suspect anyone of attempting to murder Mrs. Stanford. Instead, he theorized that someone had put strychnine in the Poland water bottle *after* Mrs. Stanford had drunk from it. That is why the time of Richmond's delivery of the bottle to the Wakelee Drug Store assumes significance. If this had not been done until the next morning, any of the eight servants present might have had an opportunity to poison the water. Callundan's theory was that a servant who was jealous of Berner's intimacy with Mrs. Stanford had wanted to arouse her suspicions of the secretary.

Callundan shared his conclusion with a *San Francisco Chronicle* reporter, saying: "I would stake my good right eye against $1 that no attempt was made to poison Mrs. Stanford."[11] Dr. Jordan also held this view, according to the *New York Times*.[12] The question of what the three women had tasted in the water was not addressed.

3 ◠ The Police Investigation

Shocking News Reaches San Francisco

It is difficult to imagine the shock Harry Morse must have felt when he read the headline stretching across the front page of the evening *San Francisco Bulletin* of March 1, 1905: "Mrs. Stanford Dies, Poisoned." The *Bulletin*'s editor, Fremont Older, was then focused on a campaign to expose graft rampant in the office of San Francisco's Mayor Eugene Schmitz. As the historian Walton Bean notes, "only the most sensational events of war or crime could take precedence over headlines charging graft in municipal affairs. The shooting of the race-track magnate, Frank T. "Caesar" Young . . . the fall of Port Arthur to the Japanese . . . the death of Mrs. Leland Stanford under extraordinary circumstances—only such events could crowd charges of municipal corruption off the *Bulletin*'s front page."[1]

Morse had followed Callundan's investigation closely and had been in regular contact with Mrs. Stanford's lawyer, Mountford Wilson. Because his agents had found no illicit purchases of strychnine in Bay Area pharmacies, had learned that Mrs. Stanford was universally loved, and had unearthed no motive for anyone to have poisoned her, Morse also had tended to subscribe to the theory that the water had been poisoned after Mrs. Stanford had drunk from the bottle, and that there had been no attempt on her life. In fact, Morse had signed off on Callundan's report to Wilson, and the case was dormant.

The newspapers were quick to criticize this casual theory, one that dismissed the statements of Mrs. Stanford, Bertha Berner, and Elizabeth Richmond that each had encountered a disagreeable, bitter taste when sampling the Poland water. In one journalist's estimation, failure "to remove all danger of another such attempt continued until it was

too late to frustrate the villainous plans of the poisoner." Word from
police headquarters was that "some one must have known long prior to
the death of Mrs. Stanford that the attempt to poison her in this city
was not an 'alleged' attempt."[2] Had the attempt been taken as seriously
as the circumstances warranted, Morse and Callundan would have seen
to the confiscation of all bottles and packets of powders in Mrs. Stanford's medicine chest.

Sheriff Henry's Confusing Cablegram

Acting San Francisco Police Chief John Spillane initiated an investigation on March 1, 1905.[3] Although confident of the efficiency of
Morse's men, Spillane was critical of Mountford Wilson for having
terminated the inconclusive investigation, and he launched his probe
without conferring with Stanford officials. Spillane put Joseph Burnett,
his captain of detectives, on the case and requested the files and con-
tinuing assistance of the Morse agency's Captain Callundan.[4] Like everyone else, Spillane hoped that the Honolulu investigation would disclose that Mrs. Stanford had died of natural causes.

That hope was shattered when, on March 2, Spillane received a cablegram from Honolulu High Sheriff William Henry that read: "The
Stanford bottle of bicarbonate of soda contained forty-three *drams*
[emphasis added] in which there were 662 grains of strychnine. Examination of organs underway. Will cable as soon as completed."[5] Reporters were stunned by how much strychnine was supposedly added to the
bicarbonate of soda—enough, they pointed out, to kill a regiment
(whereas the amount in the Poland water was said to have been sufficient only to kill twenty people). Clearly, it seemed, the poisoner had
meant business and planned not to fail a second time.

Henry wired that the results of the toxicological analyses of Mrs.
Stanford's organs would be sent shortly. When no further information
was received in San Francisco police headquarters, the press began to
suspect a cover-up. Henry reportedly denied sending the cablegram
about the bicarbonate of soda. Possibly he issued the denial, but if so, it
was more than likely to cover up his mistake than to throw doubt on
the poisoning theory, in which he firmly believed. What may have confused the sheriff were the units of measurement: the chemists had found
that the bottle contained "the total amount [of] 43 *grams* or 662
grains" of *bicarbonate of soda* (emphasis added). Henry's change of

grams to *drams* would calculate out to 1,172 grains. Wondering where the number 662 came from, he may have concluded it referred to strychnine, not total bicarbonate of soda, leading to the erroneous telegram. Thereafter, Henry gave no more information to newspapermen; they would have to wait until Mr. Robert Duncan and Dr. Edmund Shorey testified at the coroner's inquest, held on March 6, 7, and 9, 1905. As the days passed, High Sheriff Henry's reluctance to issue additional toxicological reports, indeed, his denial that he had sent the first telegram, vexed mainland newspapermen and was interpreted as collusion with the San Francisco police department and Stanford officials to cover up Mrs. Stanford's murder. Suspicions waned only after the reporters had interviewed several chemists and learned that assaying strychnine in organic tissue was a tricky and time-consuming task. Although over the next several weeks they wrote conflicting reports of the degree of cooperation and trust between the Honolulu and San Francisco police departments, it is clear that High Sheriff Henry never doubted that Mrs. Stanford had been murdered.

Witnesses Interrogated

The San Francisco police probe focused on members of the Stanford household. On the night of January 14, there had been ten individuals at the Stanford mansion, including Mrs. Stanford. Of these, only five had access to Mrs. Stanford's bedroom—Bertha Berner, Elizabeth Richmond, Nora Hopkins, Ah Wing, and Ah Young. Not surprisingly, early suspicion thus fell on Berner, who was the only witness to both poisonings. Reporters cooked up stories about her rumored intimacy with Beverly, but Spillane quickly concluded on the basis of character witnesses that she was innocent, as did Henry. Berner had been Mrs. Stanford's intimate secretary for twenty years, and they were fond of each other. She enjoyed the privilege of luxurious travel and well-compensated employment. Ending this would not have been to her advantage, the police decided.

The San Francisco police investigation was coordinated by Captain Burnett and was assisted by the Morse agency. At least six detectives were involved in the probe, which lasted only two weeks. Mountford Wilson, Charles Lathrop, and California Attorney General Lewis F. Byington also participated in interrogations of some of the suspects. These were quickly reduced to three: Richmond, Ah Wing, and Beverly.

Each was questioned repeatedly during long sessions in Burnett's office. When told she was going to the "sweat box," Richmond was said
to have had visions of "French inquisitors" and to have longed for
England. On one occasion, she endured a four-hour interrogation by
Byington, Wilson, Burnett, and two detectives. Their purpose was to
discover contradictions as she told her story over and over again. Aside
from minor details, however, her account held together well. During
one session, she recalled that the temporary butler, William McWhinney, had uncorked the bottle of Poland water that she took to Mrs.
Stanford's room on January 13. When McWhinney was questioned
about this, he opined that the police must have misunderstood Richmond, because he had not uncorked a bottle.

"Captain Burnett swung in his chair that he might give vent to ill-
suppressed laughter," the *Call* reported in the popular style of the
times.[6] But as it turned out, Richmond could not have poisoned the bicarbonate of soda; it had been purchased on February 6, 1905, ten days
after she was dismissed.

Ah Wing and Beverly underwent the same intense grilling, Ah Wing
particularly so because it was reported that Berner had named him as
the poisoner. Berner repeatedly denied this allegation, but Ah Wing
surely suffered from the false report. He was said to have lost considerable weight during the ordeal. He had served as factotum at the Stanford mansion for twenty years or more, and his gentle disposition and
devotion to Mrs. Stanford were affirmed by those who knew him. Anti-
Chinese sentiment in San Francisco in 1905 was ugly, and both the police and the press indulged in scurrilous derogatory references to
"Mongolians." In the end, after trying "to wring words from the reluctant lips," Chief Spillane concluded, "Ah Wing is a bad man and a liar
but I don't believe he had the least connection with Mrs. Stanford's
death."[7] Mrs. Stanford remembered Ah Wing in her will.

Why the suspect list included Beverly is unclear, except that some
regarded him as unscrupulous. He had left Mrs. Stanford's employment
in the summer of 1904 and had only been back to the mansion once to
confer with her, in December. Mrs. Stanford planned several dinner
parties for January 1905 and could not find an American butler as suitable as the Englishman (Beverly thought American butlers little more
than window washers). Stories circulated, however, that while traveling with Mrs. Stanford, he had helped her acquire art objects for the
Stanford museum, adding 10 percent or more to the purchase price for

himself. It was rumored, but never confirmed, that he split these profits with Berner. He told the police, however, that such commissions were perquisites of foreign travel, that "it [was] expected and nobody ever complains about it."[8] The police officials, no strangers to kickbacks and graft, cleared Mr. Beverly.

Experts Voice Opinions

Various experts rendered opinions on the case, most of which were not particularly helpful. George W. Hazen of the federal Secret Service asserted, for example, that strychnine was a woman's poison and reasoned that a deranged woman must have killed Mrs. Stanford, seeking to eliminate her control of the university budget. The police were not taken by the theory. The celebrated case of Dr. William Palmer loomed large in their minds. Palmer, the "Prince of Poisoners," had been hanged for murdering John Parsons Cook with strychnine and was memorialized in wax at Madame Tussaud's in London.[9] Palmer had blamed a bumbling physician for Cook's death, but the jury had not so found. Fresh in memory, as well, was the case of Dr. Thomas Neill Cream, who had murdered four prostitutes, and no one knew how many other people, with capsules of strychnine, which he convinced them were for the good of their health. Cream, in an elaborate blackmail scheme, had threatened to provide the police with evidence that another physician, Dr. William H. Harper, was the killer.[10] Secret Service Agent Hazen might just as well have said that strychnine was a doctor's poison.

Reporters interviewed a number of physicians and toxicologists, most of whom believed that Mrs. Stanford could not have drunk Poland water containing enough strychnine to kill "twenty persons" without having done herself serious harm, that violent convulsions and death would have been the outcome. That putative dose of strychnine originated in interviews of Mrs. Henry Highton in Honolulu, who later testified at the inquest that Mrs. Stanford had given her the information. When Mountford Wilson finally issued Louis Falkenau's assay, showing that a glass of the Poland water had contained 0.8 grains of strychnine (a dose just about right to kill someone), the medical experts grew quiet on this subject.

One medical expert, though, was quoted at some length. The *Call* reported on March 6 that "Dr. George Herbert said this morning: 'I am confident that Mrs. Stanford was poisoned by strychnine. Even if they find none in her stomach it will not disprove this fact . . . there were all the indications of strychnine poisoning in this case. The position of the body was one indication. The corpse rested on head and heels, curving upward at the stomach, and the rigor of the spine was pronounced.'"

Dr. Herbert's statement attracted no attention. The newspaper neither provided further details identifying him, as it often did other experts, nor showed any curiosity as to how he had obtained information about the posture of the body. (Clinical details of Mrs. Stanford's death and the autopsy findings had not yet been released.) It is obvious now that Dr. Humphris told him; George Herbert was his medical partner.

The celebrated newswoman Winifred Black, who had earned her reputation as a "sob sister" reporting for William Randolph Hearst's *San Francisco Examiner*, wrote that Mrs. Stanford had led an empty life since the death of her son Leland Jr. twenty years earlier, consumed by a longing to join him in the hereafter, spending fortunes on spiritual mediums, "liv[ing] in this world simply at intervals." She hoped that Mrs. Stanford had not been poisoned, but if she had, then "the person who did it held a sweeter goblet to her thirsty lips than any she has ever drunk for twenty years." Black hoped that the mediums would let Mrs. Stanford rest in peace.[11]

Mrs. Stanford's Spiritualism

Responding to reporters, President David Starr Jordan touched on the subject of Mrs. Stanford's spiritual beliefs as he prepared to board the SS *Alameda* in San Francisco and again when he arrived in Honolulu. He thought she had not been a spiritualist in the sense associated with "masks and other fancies."[12] He felt the same about Miss Berner. That a psychic message from Leland Jr. had directed Senator Stanford to found the university had frequently been suggested by the medium Maud Lord Drake. It was well known that the Stanfords had attended a Drake séance with Ulysses S. Grant, the former president, and his wife. To set the record straight, the Stanfords had asked Jordan to preserve a memorandum of their statement that spiritualism had nothing to do with the university, that "in the commercial spiritualism of the professional medium, neither . . . had a particle of faith."[13]

Nevertheless, there is no question that Mrs. Stanford suffered greatly from the loss of her son and thought of his soul as immortal. No doubt she would have desired to gain contact with him, and it is likely that she tried frequently to do so. No doubt, as well, she was frustrated and disappointed after attending sessions with fraudulent mediums. In 1903, traveling with Berner, Richmond, and Beverly, she had paid her only visit to her brother-in-law, Thomas Welton Stanford, of Melbourne, Australia. Stanford, an amateur scientist who was deeply involved in spiritism, arranged a sitting with his professional medium, Charles Baily. The latter was unable to effect a spiritualistic connection, however, quite possibly owing to inadequate information about Mrs. Stanford's loved ones.

Although not taken in by false spirit-visitations, Jordan explained, Mrs. Stanford was nevertheless anxious that scientists discover how she might communicate with her dead husband for guidance. She read widely on the subject and wished to establish a campus facility for scientific study of spiritualism, in part to further that aim.[14]

One can imagine how much she anticipated the visiting professorship of the Harvard philosopher William James, who had been a leader in psychical research in the late 1890s and remained open-minded on the subject. Just a month before her death, Mrs. Stanford told Horace Davis of an exchange she had had with President Jordan about James's planned sabbatical leave at Stanford. Jordan had complained about the freeze in Stanford faculty salaries. How, he wondered, could Mrs. Stanford recommend a stipend of $5,000 for James when Jordan could not have funds for salary increases for Professors Gilbert, Jenkins, and Marx (faculty members whom Mrs. Stanford thought of as Jordan's "pets," who were singled out for high salaries)? "My answer was—Dr. Jordan, there is only one Prof. James."[15]

Julian Hawthorne's Theory

The *San Francisco Examiner* commissioned a psychological analysis of the circumstances of Mrs. Stanford's death from the novelist Julian Hawthorne, who was famous for his interest and experience in criminology. Hawthorne prefaced his analysis by expressing relief to learn that Mrs. Stanford might not have been murdered. He then went on to develop a psychological profile of the killer(s) in an "imaginary" case, hoping to expose the reader to "less familiar divagations of human nature." There would inevitably be animosity among the subordinates of a wealthy, commanding widow who was devoid of a liberal education and addicted to spiritualism, Hawthorne said—animosities that might be "inflamed by brooding over the intellectual and other defects of the employer."

The subordinates, in Hawthorne's scenario, were "persons of some education and mental capacity," and jealousy, distrust, and conspiracies might germinate in them when they gradually discovered themselves to be in a state of bondage. In carrying out whatever was commanded by the ignorant woman, he speculated, they suffered progressive loss of self-respect, until finally "the hatred of contempt galled by the chain of servitude" set in, "the most murderous hatred of all." Hawthorne's broader intent was to attack domestic servitude, which he thought as evil as slavery, but reviewing his transparent hypothetical case, one can see that he had in mind not only Mrs. Stanford's personal servants but everyone who might be suspected of poisoning her.[16]

The police conducted a thorough search of the Stanford mansion. Many newspaper reports announced the discovery of a cache of strychnine, obviously used, they said, to poison both the Poland water and the bicarbonate of soda (reporters did not know at the time that whereas the Poland water had contained nux vomica, the bicarbonate of soda was spiked with pure strychnine). These reports were consistently denied by authorities and have no credence. In fact, the investigation uncovered no evidence against any suspect, and no arrest was ever made.

4 ⌒ The Honolulu Inquest

Eyewitness Testimony

High Sheriff Henry had hoped to convene the coroner's jury as early as March 1, but the inquest was delayed until Monday, March 6, because of the time required to complete the toxicological analyses. On March 4, David Starr Jordan embarked for Honolulu on the SS *Alameda*, along with Detective Harry Reynolds of the San Francisco police, the Morse agency's Jules Callundan, and Timothy Hopkins, a Stanford University trustee. The *Daily Palo Alto*, in announcing that Jordan would bring Mrs. Stanford's body home, reported a rumor that he had other business to attend to in Honolulu, which, although flatly denied by his secretary, George Clark, turned out indeed to be the case.[1]

In the days preceding the inquest, Deputy Sheriff Rawlins and Judge Stanley thoroughly interviewed Miss Berner and Miss Hunt and became convinced of their innocence. Judge Stanley had been retained to represent the interests of Mrs. Stanford's heirs. The judge was a leading Honolulu attorney, a partner in the law firm Holmes and Stanley, who had been appointed second judge of the First Circuit Court at the age of twenty-five, but had retired in 1900 after a three-year stint on the bench. Stanley was an Irishman (known as the "Nipper" in rugby circles) whose sharp-witted arguments once brought guffaws from stern-faced members of the U.S. Supreme Court.[2]

Stanley represented the Stanford interests with diligence. He was present when the forensic evidence was wrapped by Sheriff Rawlins and turned over to Dr. Pratt; went to the laboratory when the toxicologists analyzed the bicarbonate of soda; participated in the deposition of Miss Berner; and attended the inquest hearings, where he was not reticent about asking questions of witnesses. No record shows that he was dissatisfied with the legality, honesty, or outcome of the proceedings.

The inquest was held in the private dining rooms of the Moana Hotel. The partition separating the two rooms was folded back for the occasion and a large table was placed in the opening between the rooms to seat reporters. The inner room held Deputy Sheriff Rawlins, the coroner; Judge Stanley, who reporters noted constantly whispered to the coroner, as if prompting questions; the witness chair; two stenographers, George Sea and Henry Van Gieson; and Attorney General Lorrin Andrews. The six jurors sat scattered around the room, according to the *Pacific Commercial Advertiser* "in easily lounging attitudes—but manifesting the keenest interest in what was going forward."[3] The *San Francisco Call*, accustomed to greater formality in courtrooms, was cynical: "The jurymen, in the graceful negligee of the tropics, sat . . . in attitudes suggestive rather of personal desire than of any deep sense of gravity of the duty that called them there."[4] A few spectators wandered in and out of the outer room.

Bertha Berner was the first witness called when the proceedings began on Monday afternoon. Suspicious newsmen, forever seeking culprits, focused on the *Pacific Commercial Advertiser*'s characterization of Berner's demeanor as "frank, if anything . . . too engagingly frank." To them, she was a woman who weighed each word with infinite care, as if she had something to hide. The *Advertiser*'s fuller account, however, was clearly admiring:

Miss Berner certainly is a most remarkable woman, and showed it in no way better than in the way in which she stood the ordeal of yesterday. There were other witnesses of course, who told more thrilling stories at the inquest—but there will never be a witness heard in any case who will impress those who hear testimony more than this woman, a stranger among strangers and conscious of the possibility of hostility toward herself, who told yesterday [of] her relations to the dead woman who was her benefactress. Only when she told the actual story of death did she show any signs whatever of weakness.[5]

The official stenographers recorded Berner's testimony, much of which has been covered already, as though it were being read from a prepared statement. In the inquest report, it is printed that way—that is, there are no headings for "Q" and "A," as there are for other witnesses. After her intensive examination by Rawlins and Stanley, a prepared statement might have been advised and read into the record. The court stenographers' transcription is at times cryptic and poorly punctuated, in contrast to the *Pacific Commercial Advertiser*'s version of the testimony, which flows smoothly and indicates where questions were asked and by whom.

In fact, it was Attorney General Andrews who wanted to know how often Mrs. Stanford took bicarbonate of soda and who had known about her habit. Berner responded that bicarbonate of soda was Mrs. Stanford's favorite medicine. She had not taken a dose for many weeks (because she had been eating less since the January poisoning), but the usual frequency was about once a week. Berner, Richmond, and the housemaid Nora Hopkins were familiar with the habit. Who had brought her the Poland water in San Francisco? Richmond had brought the bottle to her bedroom, answered Berner (from the kitchen, where the bottle had been uncorked by a Chinaman, added the *Pacific Commercial Advertiser* reporter). Who had prescribed the cascara capsules? Dr. Hillman prescribed them for me, Berner replied: they were mine.

There followed a good deal of confusion over Dr. Hillman, whose name also appeared on the Wakelee label of the cascara bottle, dated October 25, 1901. When the *San Francisco Chronicle* sent a reporter to interview the doctor, he found that there were only two Drs. Hillman in the United States, one in Kentucky, and one in rural New York. It is possible that the cascara was prescribed by Dr. Stanley *Stillman*, professor of surgery at the Cooper Medical College, brother of John Maxson Stillman, professor of chemistry at Stanford University, and son of Leland Stanford's friend Dr. J. D. B. Stillman.

The *Pacific Commercial Advertiser* credited Berner with two important elements of testimony that oddly enough never found their way into the corner's inquest report. First was her description of how she had spooned the bicarbonate of soda from its container: "I put in the spoon, tilting the bottle a little, and dipped out the soda. I think I did not let the soda pile up on one side when I tipped the bottle . . . I dipped the soda right out, probably from the top, but I am not sure on this point."[6] Whether the stenographers could not keep up with the tilting, dipping, and tipping, or thought these details unworthy of memorializing, is not known, but the issue of dispersion of the strychnine in the soda—the homogeneity of the mixture—came up the following day when the toxicologists testified.

Also not recorded in the official transcript was Berner's observation while rubbing Mrs. Stanford's back that she was in a state of "profuse perspiration." The reader will recall that Dr. Murray had commented that Mrs. Stanford's body felt hot. An elevated temperature and sweating would be expected as a result of the intense muscular contractions caused by strychnine. Otherwise, the journalist's and stenographers' reports agree.

Dr. Clifford Brown Wood testified next. He described the findings of the autopsy, the report of which did not include a cause of death pending toxicology, and stressed that there were no morbid findings diagnostic of strychnine poisoning. But, he added, "the post mortem appearances . . . in known cases of strychnia poisoning correspond with the post mortem appearances which were found at this autopsy. The other important thing for the jury to know is that an examination of the different organs of the body, and they were all examined, failed to show any sufficient cause of death."[7] Dr. Day, whose testimony closed the afternoon session, agreed fully with Wood's assessment and conclusions:

Q. And in your opinion there was no cause or any reason to lead you to believe that Mrs. Stanford died from natural causes?
A. Not that I found, I saw none.

During the evening session, Rawlins took the testimony of Drs. Murray and Humphris, and May Hunt. Murray, a Canadian, did not hesitate to declare his diagnosis: "Had I been called without any one telling me anything else than that she had been taken sick twenty minutes before . . . and I found her in that condition, just dying, or in the spasm, or dead, I would have suspected strychnia at once." Humphris, an Englishman (soon to be described by Dr. Jordan as a "man without professional or personal standing"[8]), recited his medical credentials at the request of Coroner Rawlins: "Doctor of Medicine, Doctor of Surgery, Fellow of the Royal College of Physicians of Edinburgh, Member of the Royal College of Surgeons of England, Licentiate of the Royal College of Physicians of London, etc." He had practiced in Hawaii for seven years; he had seen cases of strychnine poisoning, both fatal and nonfatal. "The spasm is so typical," he emphasized, "that there is only one other thing which could be mistaken for it . . . tetanus, or lock-jaw as it is commonly known," easily eliminated from consideration in Mrs. Stanford's case by the absence of a wound and the dramatically rapid course.

Humphris added his personal observations of the autopsy. When the thorax was opened, he was struck that the heart and lungs were displaced by a contracted diaphragm. Like other muscles, the diaphragm lingered in the spasm that had caused respiratory paralysis and death

by asphyxia. He also pointed out that there was no food in the stomach, only water. To consider "acute indigestion" as a cause of death
(mainland newspapers had proffered that diagnosis) would be absurd,
he said. Coroner Rawlins pushed him:

Q. And what in your opinion was the cause of death?
A. She died of strychnia poisoning.
Q. She died of strychnia poisoning?
A. Absolutely.

Hunt was the final witness that evening, giving testimony that
agreed in every detail with that of other pertinent witnesses, corrobo-
rating Berner's account of packing at the Nob Hill mansion for the trip
to Honolulu. Hunt, although she had known Mrs. Stanford for several
years, had come into her employ on February 9, 1905, as a replacement
for Elizabeth Richmond. She pointed out that Mrs. Stanford's various
medicines, including the bottle of bicarbonate of soda, sat on a table in
the room where the packing took place from February 9, at least, to
February 14, when the medicine basket was taken to the steamship.

During this interval, the room was open every day and was largely
unattended. The bottle of bicarbonate of soda was accessible to anyone
who entered the house. Where the medicine had been purchased, a
topic of considerable speculation in the newspapers, was immaterial—
anyone in the house could have dropped strychnine into the soda,
whatever its origins.

Hunt ended the evening's testimony by saying how happy Mrs. Stanford had been on the day of her death, how much she had looked forward to visiting Japan.

The Toxicologists' Testimony

On March 7, Robert Duncan and Dr. Edmund Shorey rode out to the
Moana Hotel to give the jurors their toxicological evidence, the absence
of which had promoted an unusual flood of rumors of cover-up, reported to have been planned in mysterious late-night conferences—"the
telephones at the police station and the newspaper offices nearly jingled
themselves out of order with their queries of people who had heard
fresh rumors," wrote one reporter.[9] Duncan and Shorey had worked together for many hours to extract, purify, and quantify strychnine from
the medications and from Mrs. Stanford's organs. They also performed
qualitative tests (each of which was negative) on the drinking glass,

spoon, bottles of mineral water, and a small flask of alcohol that Rawlins had marked as evidence. At the end of the day, even though the chemists' testimony was straightforward and consistent, it did not dispose of all doubts about the diagnosis. It was open to different interpretations, although the jury surely focused on Duncan's key statement, "strychnia is a foreign substance in bicarbonate of soda."

Duncan started the toxicological testimony, and Shorey finished it. There were no points of disagreement. Duncan had started to test the bicarbonate of soda early on the morning of March 1 but had abandoned the effort when called to attend Mrs. Stanford's autopsy. At noon, he had returned to his laboratory with her organs and body fluids in his possession and secured the autopsy materials in an adjacent room, which was kept locked and under police guard. Shorey had joined Duncan at the laboratory late in the day. They planned their analytical approach over supper and began the multiple analyses in earnest at 6:30 P.M. on March 1. They finished at 7 P.M. on March 4.

The chemists first analyzed the bicarbonate of soda, of which Duncan had removed a ten-gram sample that morning. The bottle containing the soda was labeled "Bicarbonate of Soda, Chas. Wells and Co. Chemist, 60 King Williams Street, Adelaide." It was a small, wide-mouthed bottle that Mrs. Stanford had kept from her trip to Australia in 1903 and had refilled with bicarbonate of soda as required. "The bottle contained 43 grams, or 662 grains" of soda, Duncan informed the jury, setting straight the confusion over weights and measures. He had deposited his morning sample (here called sample 1) in a beaker containing 100 milliliters of cold water, in which strychnine is very poorly soluble.

That evening, observing precipitates at the bottom of the beaker, he and Shorey collected the crystals on filter paper (the crystals were large enough to be picked up with fine forceps and were easily distinguished from the soda), dried them, and recorded their weight as 7/100 of a grain. Aware that Duncan's analytical method might have resulted in an underestimate, Shorey extracted two additional samples by shaking a lightly acidified solution of bicarbonate of soda with chloroform, in which strychnine is highly soluble. The chloroform was then evaporated to dryness and the procedure was repeated several times. The residual crystals were washed in water, dried, and weighed.

The second sample was taken from the bicarbonate of soda after the chemists had poured it out of the bottle into a weighing boat; the third was taken after they had thoroughly mixed the soda. These samples contained the same amount of strychnine, within the margin of error of measurement—13/100 of a grain and 14/100 of a grain, respectively. All three samples tested positively for strychnine by taste, microscopic appearance of octahedral crystals, and characteristic precipitations with platinum chloride and potassium ferricyanide. The chemists found no other alkaloids. The strychnine was pure, not rodent-grade. Duncan held up two watch glasses containing the strychnine crystals found in the bicarbonate of soda—a *foreign* substance, he emphasized, as the jurors eyed the poison.

Why did sample 1 yield a different quantity of strychnine from samples 2 and 3? Could the difference in testing methodology account for the lower amount in sample 1? Or was the difference evidence of lack of homogeneity of the mixture of poison and soda? The possibility of inhomogeneity was raised by Coroner Rawlins, who asked the chemists about the expected disposition of strychnine crystals, mixed with bicarbonate of soda, after the bottle had been agitated by movement. Both testified that the larger strychnine crystals would remain on top and the soda would sift down to the bottom. (Rawlins actually performed this experiment to his satisfaction, using sugar instead of strychnine.)

Berner believed that she had taken the soda from the top center of the bottle, perhaps tilting it a little as she did so. Unfortunately, in his early morning zeal, Duncan did not inspect the surface of the bicarbonate of soda before dipping into it. In consequence, as pointed out by Dr. Humphris when he was recalled to the stand on March 9 and asked how such a small dose could prove fatal:

I think we have no evidence to show what dose Mrs. Stanford took. Mind you, she has a bottle which we know contains more or less strychnia; we don't know that that has been thoroughly well mixed before she took it. Let us suppose for an instant that someone wished to put strychnia into that bottle, they may have dropped it in, probably hurriedly into the top; it would have fallen into the middle of the bottle, and the first dose taken out of that, the teaspoonful, would have fetched out a heavy lot of strychnia that night it was given to Mrs. Stanford, and that which was left in the bottle which the chemists found would be that sprinkling around the outside.

It was an important issue that could not be resolved.[10]

The analyses of the soda were thorough and took time—acidifying, extracting, drying, washing, and redrying repeatedly to obtain a pure chemical compound that could be weighed. The real task, however, was measuring strychnine in organic tissue, where the procedures were much more complex and involved many more steps. The chemists had been given a large number of specimens—vomitus, urine, stomach contents, intestinal contents, stomach, intestines, kidneys and liver. They first tested aliquots of each specimen separately. They found no weighable precipitate in any sample, and a color reaction for strychnine developed only in the residue of the intestinal contents.

The next step, a standard toxicological procedure that nonetheless may have shocked the jurors and reporters, was to combine, mince, and homogenize together all of the remains of Mrs. Stanford in the chemists' possession, all of those fluids and organs mentioned above. Repeated simmering and cooling, shaking with alcohol and chloroform, washing and drying, the methods standardized over the years by leading chemists, also failed to yield a weighable deposit of crystals from the voluminous homogenate. The residue did give the color reaction, the "fading purple test," when sulfuric acid and potassium bichromate were added—a procession of hues going from "the rich blue of the Orleans plum . . . to the darker purple of the mulberry and [lastly to] the bright clear red of the sweet orange, [a reaction] belong[ing] to no other substance known save strychnine."[11]

Finally, the chemists turned their attention to the cascara capsules. Not surprisingly, they detected the alkaloids brucine and strychnine. Blending nux vomica and cascara, a powder made from the bark of buckthorn trees, produced the popular medicinal capsules taken for digestive disorders. They estimated that each capsule contained one-thirtieth of a grain of strychnine, certainly a standard medicinal dose, yet one that added to Mrs. Stanford's total burden of poison.

Holding an advanced degree in chemistry from Queen's University in Kingston, Ontario, Dr. Shorey was an experienced and meticulous, if somewhat rigid, analytical chemist. He was incapable of certifying the existence of a substance that was impalpable or invisible. When asked whether he had found strychnine in the organs, he measured his words: "I don't feel justified in testifying to the presence of a thing that I cannot see or weigh, but at the same time . . . there is no other body known that gives that reaction [fading purple] . . . and that therefore it must be present in very minute quantities." He agreed with Duncan that the color reaction was so sensitive that cascara alone could account for it, an important point that Judge Stanley had raised, though it did not address the presence of strychnine in the bicarbonate of soda taken by Mrs. Stanford.

Shorey's judgment as to what constituted a significant presence of strychnine did not accord with the views of some poison experts. An authoritative contemporary work, discussing the same analytical procedures employed by Duncan and Shorey, cautions: "Should search be made for minute portions of strychnine in the tissues, considering the small amount of the poison which may produce death, it is absolutely necessary to operate on a very large quantity of material." It is advisable, it stresses, to combine not only those organs the chemists had assayed, but also the brain, spinal cord, spleen, blood, and a considerable quantity of muscle, as much as twelve percent of the whole body diced and boiled in "capacious flasks."[12]

Alfred Swaine Taylor, a leading forensic expert, was more direct. "To assert that the minutest quantity of this poison can always, and under all circumstances, be detected in the solids and fluids of the human body, because an almost infinitesimal quantity can be detected *out* of it [the body]," Taylor declares, "is not merely a simple absurdity, but an untruthful statement, calculated to mislead a jury and to deceive the public."[13] Small but lethal quantities "would be beyond the reach of a chemical analysis."[14] Dr. Shorey would later be accused of making untruthful statements, but the accuser did not have in mind the Taylor dogma.[15]

Following the brief testimony of Dr. Pratt, who verified the handling of the specimens, and a break for supper, Coroner Rawlins recalled Humphris, Murray, and Wood. The thrust of Rawlins's questions to the physicians had to do with the absorption, distribution, detection, and safety of strychnine. Absorption would be faster and more complete from a stomach full of water rather than food; distribution would be throughout the body water, estimated by Humphris at 160 lbs.; detection (except for the color test) would be difficult given the dilution, as forensic texts pointed out; and the administration of strychnine carried risks in the elderly as in the young. One-sixteenth of a grain was known to have killed a two-year-old child, both Wood and Murray testified. Murray was explicit:

Q. In administering strychnine as a medicine to patients would the age of the patient . . . govern you in regard to . . . the amount that you would give to the patient?

A. In a case of advanced age the same as a child of two or three years of age probably.

The chemists estimated that Mrs. Stanford had taken one-twelfth of a grain of strychnine. If her dose of soda had been a teaspoonful, as Hunt thought, she had taken one-eighth of a grain. If the strychnine had been concentrated at the top of the bottle, she had taken more.

The Question of Suicide

At the evening session, Dr. Humphris was also asked about Mrs. Stanford's state of mind and about the possibility of suicide. He related that when he had met her the day after her arrival, she had seemed "particularly bright and cheerful." She had been enthusiastic about going on to Japan to engage with Stanford University alumni, always one of her great pleasures wherever she traveled. Humphris admitted he had not even contemplated the possibility that she had committed suicide, but he was quick to add that now, "having considered it I should dismiss it . . . absolutely." Both Berner and Hunt had also testified that the thought of suicide had been abhorrent to Mrs. Stanford. In fact, Hunt recalled Mrs. Stanford's dread that had she been killed on January 14, it might have been thought she took her own life.

Even so, that Mrs. Stanford might have committed suicide was widely speculated in the newspapers, whose reporters sought out numerous of her friends for opinions on the possibility. All of them found it unthinkable. It was probably Lalla Highton who first planted the suspicion. Mrs. Highton wasted no time in revealing to reporters the substance of a conversation she had held with Mrs. Stanford on the lanai of the Moana Hotel.[16] The ladies had known each other for more than thirty years, and Mrs. Highton had paid a social call, unaware of the circumstances that brought Mrs. Stanford to Honolulu. Highton gave a number of newspaper interviews in which she was quoted as saying that Mrs. Stanford wept while relating the attempted poisoning in San Francisco—with enough strychnine to kill twenty persons, Highton was told, administered, Mrs. Stanford suspected, by a servant in the household.

The reporters were already aware, of course, of the Poland water episode. It was Highton's dramatic disclosure of Mrs. Stanford's talk of spiritualism that caught their attention: "We had been talking of spiritualism . . . and I sought to disabuse Mrs. Stanford's mind of the idea [the poisoning] that seemed to possess it."[17] Highton had attempted to comfort Mrs. Stanford during subsequent visits, she claimed extravagantly, by reading soothing lines of poetry. But it was the journalists' easy extrapolation of "spiritualism" to "spiritual visitations and spiritual companionship" that led the men and women of the press to the idea of suicide.[18]

Mrs. Highton's press coverage also caught the attention of Coroner Rawlins who called her to testify at the inquest on the afternoon of March 7. Highton was unable to shed any light on Mrs. Stanford's death. In fact, she admitted under oath that she had met with Mrs. Stanford only once in Honolulu, on Friday, February 24, and had always found Mrs. Stanford out driving or resting when she called subsequently. They had talked about "abstract questions," about mortality and mind power and other topics in which "she was peculiarly interested."

Then Mrs. Stanford told her about the Poland water incident. Members of the household were said to be under investigation, and Mrs. Stanford had admonished Highton, "Don't say a word about it to anybody." But Highton could not contain her alarm that Mrs. Stanford was mentally deranged, even delusional, and she rushed home to tell her husband Henry.[19] (On March 1, Mrs. Highton also mailed a full account of her encounter with Mrs. Stanford to John D. Spreckels, editor of the *San Francisco Call*.) She may have felt disappointment when Coroner Rawlins did not ask *her* about possible suicide.

On March 8, the day after Highton's testimony, the *San Francisco Call* ran a puzzling story, said to be based on an Associated Press dispatch from Honolulu, that contained new details bearing on the issue of suicide. According to the *Call*, Attorney General Andrews and Deputy Sheriff Rawlins (who had jurisdiction over the inquest) had clashed on March 6, in the course of Rawlins's questioning of Bertha Berner. Over the coroner's repeated objections, Andrews had persistently interposed questions, so the paper said, to explore the possibility that "the aged woman committed suicide." Did Mrs. Stanford complain of a bitter taste? Were the tongue and pharynx examined for the presence of strychnine? Was she "a victim of a peculiar mania?"[20] The attorney general's questions were said by the *Call* to have raised much comment in Honolulu, but, curiously, they appeared neither in the inquest report nor in the text of the hearings published in the *Pacific Commercial Advertiser*. In each account, it was Rawlins who had questioned Berner about suicide.

The Jury's Verdict

March 8 was a day off for the jurors, a day for Coroner Rawlins to digest the evidence and ask himself if he had unanswered questions. It may also have been the day W. H. Nelson disclosed to the police his suspicions that Miss Berner had concealed the poison in her parasol. He had been at the end of the pier at the same time as the Stanford party, two days before Mrs. Stanford's death, and he had witnessed a mysterious transaction, which he thought required police investigation. Berner had surreptitiously dropped an object into her collapsed parasol and given it to Hunt, who had carried it off. As a result of Mr. Nelson's disclosure, the jury was called back on March 9 to hear testimony about this episode. Berner, who seemed relieved to be questioned on such a trivial matter alone, told the jurors she had merely dropped her gloves in her parasol and asked Hunt, who was on her way to the hotel, to return the parasol to their room. Hunt gave the same account, and the inquest testimony concluded.

After handing around transcripts to be signed by the witnesses, Deputy Sheriff Rawlins cleared the dining rooms and sequestered the jury. In two minutes, little more than the time needed to write out the verdict, the jury had completed its deliberations. Rawlins read their verdict from a slip of paper the foreman placed on the table; he then translated the words into legal language, written in his own handwriting on the official coroner's inquest verdict form:

[T]he Jurors . . . upon their oaths do say that said Jane Lathrop Stanford came to her death at Honolulu, Island of Oahu, Territory of Hawaii on the twenty-eighth day of February, A.D. 1905 from strychnine poisoning, said strychnine having been introduced into a bottle of bicarbonate of soda with felonious intent by some person or persons to this jury unknown and of the contents of which bottle Jane Lathrop Stanford had partaken.

5 ⌒ The Stanford Party in Honolulu

Captain Callundan Investigates

"Mrs. Stanford Was Murdered," ran the headline greeting the Stanford party when it arrived on the *Alameda* on March 10.[1] Reporters motored out to the steamer to notify Dr. Jordan, Mr. Hopkins, and the detectives even before the ship entered the harbor. Jordan launched his own investigation of Mrs. Stanford's death shortly after his arrival in Honolulu, but he did not, in fact, attend the inquest, notwithstanding several claims to that effect.

No evidence survives of exactly what steps the Stanford party took to conduct the investigation, which concluded four days later with Jordan's categorical declaration that Mrs. Stanford had died of natural causes. Seen ashore by a reporter at noon, Jordan was asked if there were new developments and was said to have replied: "No; that matter is being taken up entirely by Mr. Hopkins and the detectives. I'm not a detective, you know—that is not part of my education."[2] The same reporter had already traced the activities of Captain Callundan and Detective Reynolds from a two-hour meeting with Berner and Hunt shortly after they disembarked to a late morning meeting with High Sheriff Henry and Attorney General Andrews, which included a pleasant reunion with former San Francisco colleagues. The detectives also arranged to move Berner and Hunt to the Alexander Young Hotel, where the Stanford party were staying. Their business concluded by noon, Callundan and Reynolds toured Chinatown.

Reporters tried to discover what it was the detectives were investigating but most of the time found them strolling around town seeing Honolulu's sights, or supervising the collection of official documents to take back to San Francisco, including transcriptions of the inquest testimony. The *Evening Bulletin* did get wind of a late night interview of Drs. Wood and Day on March 13, which had been transcribed by an "expert stenographer." According to the *Bulletin* report, the physicians had not budged from their diagnosis.[3]

Callundan later stated that he had interviewed everyone connected with the case and appended the transcribed interviews to his report to Mountford Wilson, who shared them only with Charles Lathrop. No one else, the detective said, had seen his report, including Dr. Jordan.[4] There is no doubt, however, that Jordan incorporated Callundan's findings into the press release he issued at the time of his departure from Honolulu. It is not known whether he was present during Callundan's interview of Dr. Humphris. Somehow, Jordan developed such a negative opinion of the latter that he was led to hypothesize that Humphris had *invented* the diagnosis of strychnine poisoning. Whether Jordan's low opinion of Humphris's professionalism had an experiential basis or grew out of conversations with Callundan is an intriguing question, and although it remains unanswerable, its validity can nonetheless be examined.

Dr. Waterhouse Contacted

Shortly after his arrival in Honolulu, Jordan contacted Dr. Ernest Coniston Waterhouse, sent him the autopsy and coroner's inquest reports, and requested his opinion of the circumstances of Mrs. Stanford's demise. How Waterhouse was chosen for the consultation is not certain, but he may have been recommended by the Honorable Carl S. Smith, a Stanford alumnus with whom Jordan had exchanged cables before his departure. When Jordan later submitted the consultant's bill to the Stanford executors, he indicated that Smith thought very highly of Waterhouse.

Waterhouse was a young surgeon from Honolulu who had been in private practice for just over a year. He had received his bachelor's degree from Princeton in 1894 and his medical degree from the College of Physicians and Surgeons of Columbia University in 1898. After an internship at the General Memorial Hospital in Manhattan, he returned to Honolulu to begin practice, at first as a staff surgeon at Queen's Hospital, and then, in late 1903, in partnership with Dr. James Robert Judd.[5] It would be unusual if after sixteen months of private practice, Waterhouse had attained a professional reputation on the mainland. As he wrote in his decennial Princeton class record, "I have no special achievements to report, but have been working steadily along . . . and have built up a pretty good practice."[6]

Jordan might also have sought a recommendation from the Honolulu medical patriarch Dr. John McGrew, father of John Tarn McGrew, a favorite alumnus of Mrs. Stanford, who had with other alumni organized a splendid banquet dinner for her when she stayed at the Moana Hotel in 1902.[7] Or perhaps Waterhouse was suggested by Dr. Charles B. Cooper, Dr. McGrew's son-in-law, whose wife also attended Stanford briefly.

Cooper and Waterhouse were fellow house surgeons at Queen's Hospital, and it is probable that Jordan met Cooper at the time of his meeting with D. L. Van Dine, a Stanford alumnus and entomologist at the Hawaii Agricultural Experiment Station, sometime during the weekend of his arrival.[8] At that meeting (quite likely the other business rumored by the *Daily Palo Alto*), Jordan discussed mosquito control and outlined an experiment to import mosquito fish to the islands.

Who recommended Dr. Waterhouse is not important—he was "the ablest physician we found available," Dr. Jordan wrote many years later, apparently well satisfied with the consultation.[9] Waterhouse's four-page report is entitled "Testimony of Dr. Waterhouse."[10] It began with answers to three leading questions, framed almost certainly by Jordan:[11]

Q. Considering the symptoms, without regard to the fact that strychnine was found to be present in the contents of the intestine, would you be willing to say that Mrs. Stanford died of strychnine poisoning?
A. Decidedly not.
Q. Was there any possibility of the death of Mrs. Stanford being due to angina pectoris or anything other than strychnine poisoning?
A. Yes.
Q. Considering the fact that strychnine was found in traces in the contents of the intestine, would that fact change your answers to questions 1 and 2?
A. No.

There was much more to the analysis, of course, and it calls for closer examination. Waterhouse thought further distribution of his report should be at Jordan's discretion if he were to "find it of any service whatever in anything more than a private way, though in all probability there is no further use you would have for it."[12] One infers that Waterhouse would, in fact, have preferred that the report not be released. Although as far as is known, the "testimony" was shared only with Mountford Wilson, who coordinated the investigation, Jordan often referred to the Waterhouse report in both private and official correspondence and in his memoirs, and he relied on it for proof that Mrs. Stanford had died as a result of "rupture of the coronary artery."

The body of Waterhouse's report said nothing about the treatment given Mrs. Stanford by Dr. Humphris. These criticisms were covered in a letter to Dr. Jordan that accompanied the report. Why had Dr. Humphris not put Mrs. Stanford to bed? Why had he allowed Miss Berner and Miss Hunt to keep rubbing her? Why did he permit the use of counterirritants up to the very end? "I have purposely left out anything whatever in the way of criticism of any doctor connected with the case," Waterhouse wrote, "with the exception of course of what can be read between the lines." Although Humphris eventually become aware of the report, whether he also learned of Waterhouse's criticisms of his actions is unknown. The two physicians appear to have maintained something of a professional relationship at meetings of the Hawaiian Territorial Medical Society. Waterhouse's comments on research papers delivered by Humphris tended toward sarcasm, but that may have been his usual manner.

Dr. Waterhouse's Opinion

The thrust of Dr. Waterhouse's opinion was that Mrs. Stanford had not exhibited symptoms of strychnine poisoning: "I fail to find one characteristic symptom of strychnine poisoning." Had she been thrown out of bed by a strychnine convulsion, not only would she have been unable to walk to the door but, more important, would have been intolerant of the ministrations of Berner and Hunt. Their rubbing and bathing of Mrs. Stanford's hands and feet "would set a patient suffering from strychnine poisoning nearly wild," Waterhouse maintained, "the slightest external irritation setting her off into another convulsion." Unlike the spasm that took Mrs. Stanford's life, a strychnine seizure, he believed, would cause muscle twitching, violent convulsions, opisthotonos (arching of the back), rigid abdominal and thoracic muscles, staring eyes, and risus sardonicus (an involuntary grin from contraction of facial muscles).

After citing the classic animal experiments of the physiologist Claude Bernard and others to reinforce his point that sensory stimulation triggers violent convulsions in someone poisoned with strychnine,

Waterhouse formulated his diagnosis. In his view, "all the symptoms enumerated by those witnessing them, up to the spasm at the time of death, read from the evidence like those of hysteria." A hysterical spasm could have thrown Mrs. Stanford out of bed. Alternatively, her *claim* of ejection could have been simply a melodramatic exaggeration. The complaint that her jaws were set was clearly emotional, because Berner did not describe muscle rigidity. (Waterhouse did not comment on the spasm of the masseter muscles palpated by Humphris.) Even Mrs. Stanford's *calling attention* to her stiff jaws Waterhouse interpreted as hysterical.

Her exclamations, "I am so sick," "I have no control of my body," "I think I am poisoned again," were not the complaints expected of a victim of strychnine poisoning. "If this had been a typical strychnine poisoning convulsion she would have known she was poisoned— nothing is more frightful," Waterhouse wrote, disregarding Mrs. Stanford's final utterance: "This is a horrible death to die."

In Dr. Waterhouse's diagnostic formulation, it was Mrs. Stanford's hysterical panic, her stomach distended from indigestion and her body exhausted from undue exertion, which led to her demise "from fatty heart or myocarditis or angina pectoris." Sometimes chest pain is not prominent, he pointed out, and the preconceived theory of strychnine poisoning held by Dr. Clifford Brown Wood, the pathologist brought in by Humphris, might have caused him to overlook meaningful cardiac pathology. Alternatively, he added, paraphrasing Professor Francis Delafield of Columbia University, whose text he had consulted, "in some of the fatal cases of angina pectoris no lesion of the heart or arteries are [*sic*] found." In postulating a cardiac death, Waterhouse did not trouble to explain the pathogenesis of the contorting spasm suffered by Mrs. Stanford, not a phenomenon of fatal angina pectoris, or comment on the presence of cyanotic blood in the chambers of the heart, not an indication of sudden cardiac arrest.

Could Dr. Waterhouse have thought that Mrs. Stanford unconsciously mimed the spasm of strychnine poisoning during an attack of hysteria? The convulsive features of hysteria were well known to medical students of Waterhouse's generation. W. R. Gowers's *Diseases of the Nervous System* reproduced Paul Richer's famous drawings of different phases of "hysteria major," sketches of young women afflicted by what was called the "phase of contortions."[13] Various spasmodic postures (including opisthotonos) developed in patients in the throes of an attack, and Waterhouse might not have given Mrs. Stanford's spasm a second thought.

It was a time when a diagnosis of hysteria easily crossed the minds of physicians blind-sided by male chauvinism, as was Dr. Waterhouse. Just another hysterical old woman, he may have thought, aligning himself with the diagnostician discussed in the standard reference work *Poisons, Their Effects and Detection* who was "so possessed with the view that the case was due to hysteria, that, even after making the post-mortem examination, and finding no adequate lesion, he theorized as to the possibility of some fatal hysteric spasm of the glottis, while there was ample chemical evidence of strychnine."[14]

Waterhouse attached no significance to the marked rigidity of Mrs. Stanford's body described by the pathologist. As he correctly argued, the autopsy was performed at a time when postmortem rigidity normally developed. He failed altogether to see the significant point that Mrs. Stanford's rigidity had been present from the moment of her death, preserving the attitudes of the wrenching spasm that took her life. As Francis Delafield says of normal postmortem rigor: "Death is usually succeeded immediately by a period of complete muscular relaxation. . . . On the occurrence of rigor mortis the muscles [then] become fixed in whatever position they may have had *at the time of its occurrence* [emphasis added]."[15]

Dr. Waterhouse's report contained details that might help prove his points but did not appear in the testimony. For instance, whereas Humphris called attention to involuntary tight fisting during the final spasm, Waterhouse wrote, "Mrs. Stanford simply grips Miss Berner's hands more tightly . . . and finally Mrs. Stanford's head falls to the side just as Miss Berner disengages one hand to hold Mrs. Stanford's head from falling."[16] Aside from the fact that nowhere in the testimony are such actions described, the consultant simply ignored the spasmodic extension of the head testified to by Humphris and Murray. Just at the moment of death, Waterhouse continued, Mrs. Stanford had exclaimed, "Oh! Oh! Oh!" indicating to him that the expected contraction of facial muscles, the risus sardonicus, was not present. But those were not words attributed to Mrs. Stanford at the inquest.

Dr. Waterhouse based much of his report on his private interrogation of Miss Berner. From his account, it appears that Berner had started to change her inquest testimony, from which she would veer strongly much later in her memoir.

Shortly after departing Honolulu on the SS *Alameda*, Jordan dashed off a note to Waterhouse instructing him to send a copy of Berner's written answers to his questions. There was not much to send; Waterhouse had not kept notes. "As you will see," he responded, "her answers in the written statement are not nearly so full and complete . . . not realizing what were the especial things I wanted to know, in answering again at her leisure she naturally often left out the point I wished to find out about."

He had not known that Dr. Jordan wanted to preserve these questions and answers, but he took the opportunity to reinforce his earlier points by reviewing Mrs. Stanford's posture at the moment of her death. "The turning in of the soles of the feet . . . the nearest approach to a characteristic symptom" meant little, Waterhouse commented defensively, in view of the fact that "the angle between the body and thighs [was] not obliterated."[17] Any second thoughts he might have had notwithstanding, as Mrs. Stanford expired sitting in a chair, her legs were not extended as in the classic textbook picture in his mind.

One written response from Berner had to do with Mrs. Stanford's exclamation that she had been thrown from her bed by a spasm. Berner wrote that in her belief, Mrs. Stanford "[did] not mean that the spasm threw her out of bed and down on the floor . . . because I know how very difficult it would have been for Mrs. Stanford to have risen alone." For years, she had avoided sitting in low chairs and taking tub baths because she was unable to arise from them.[18] It evidently did not occur to Waterhouse that such prominent weakness of the extensor muscles of Mrs. Stanford's lower extremities (sometimes mistakenly called menopausal myopathy) might preclude the final posture he thought mandatory to diagnose strychnine poisoning, a posture that in simple terms is determined by the stronger muscle acting across a joint—in Mrs. Stanford's case, her flexor muscles.

Dr. Waterhouse's Limitations

Asserting that a woman of Mrs. Stanford's age suffered from hysteria was an entirely unacceptable diagnosis in the opinion of W. R. Gowers, a prominent nineteenth-century authority on nervous diseases.[19] Dr. Waterhouse did raise reasonable objections to the diagnosis of strychnine poisoning. His clinical perceptions, however, were those of a reviewer of documents who had glanced at classical textbooks to strengthen his diagnosis—Taylor on poisons, Delafield on pathology—and not those of an attending physician or a witness to the death. The problem was that he saw only a full-blown textbook picture, a gestalt.

He did not conceive of progressing stages of strychnine poisoning: early apprehension and insecurity of gait ("I have no control of my body," Mrs. Stanford had exclaimed), advancement to muscular stiffness and premonition of death, and termination in a fatal tetanic spasm. He did not appear to consider dose and sensitivity (indeed, his report contains no mention whatever of strychnine in the bicarbonate of soda), and he did not pose the question of whether a small dose of the poison could kill yet be insufficient to cause the powerful axial muscle contractions that resulted in the opisthotonos of his textbooks. He was not yet a seasoned clinician, and it seems unlikely that he was writing from the perspective of personal experience.

The experienced clinician does not require the whole syndrome in order to make a diagnosis, does not deny Parkinson's disease, to use a familiar example, because of the absence of a tremor. Beginning doctors read that patients with Parkinson's disease show resting tremor, bradykinesia, cog wheel rigidity, masked facies, flexed posture, stammering speech, and shuffling gait. They would scarcely dare diagnose the disorder, as could the preeminent neurologist S. A. Kinnier Wilson, solely on the basis of "muscular impatience" of the legs, a diagnosis Wilson would confirm by the progression of symptoms.[20] In any neurological disorder early diagnosis is more difficult than late; progression of symptoms provides important clues. But if strychnine is detected in the dead body, the toxicologist Alfred Swaine Taylor says, "the symptoms in their commencement, progress and termination will furnish irrefragable proof that it has acted as a poison."[21]

Had he had the resources (Queen's Hospital did not have a medical library in 1905) and the inclination, Waterhouse could have developed a broader understanding of strychnine poisoning. He would have discovered the extraordinary variability from case to case: alarming symptoms developing after one-sixteenth of a grain;[22] and little more than an unsteady gait, followed by recovery, after eight grains.[23] He would have encountered descriptions of Mrs. Stanford's terminal symptoms: the "sense of impending death . . . eyeballs prominent and pupils dilated . . . inability to drink from spasms of jaws . . . respiration suspended during convulsion . . . patient quite conscious."[24] He might even have found reports of patients thrown out of bed by a spasm.

Dr. Waterhouse, although correct in his conviction that a slight brush or draught might evoke a spasm, would have learned that patients poisoned with strychnine often experience a sense of great relief when rubbed, that a firm grasp does not trigger a convulsive spasm.[25] As Thomas Hawkes Tanner says, the patient "begs for help, and perhaps asks to be held, or rubbed,"[26] treatment recognized years later in an editorial of the *Journal of the American Medical Association*— "gradual, steady movements for which the patient is prepared are harmless, and gentle soothing handling and reassurance of the patient are fairly effective in mitigating even the established spasms."[27] Bertha Berner and May Hunt had served their mistress caringly and correctly during her final moments. Dr. Humphris had acted professionally.[28]

Dr. Jordan's Conclusion

Dr. Jordan and Dr. Waterhouse met over dinner at the University Club on Monday evening, March 13 (Dr. Day also dined at the club that evening), to discuss the content of the report. It was at this meeting that the decision was taken to consider it a privileged communication. It would be up to Jordan to use Waterhouse's opinions on Mrs. Stanford's death as he saw fit. Jordan received the final report on March 14. That same day, a dispatch to the *New York Times* disclosed that Dr. Jordan, as a doctor of medicine, had made up his mind: Mrs. Stanford had not died of strychnine poisoning. The dose she had taken was medicinal.[29] Jordan drafted a press statement on Alexander Young Hotel stationary for release the next day, and he asked Timothy Hopkins to sign it.

At 9:00 A.M. on March 15, 1905, the Stanford party, Stanford alumni, and many prominent citizens of Honolulu attended funeral services for Mrs. Stanford at the Central Union Church. Jordan and Hopkins served as pallbearers, together with Governor Carter, district officials, and Delos Van Dine and the Honorable Carl S. Smith, alumni of Stanford University. Carl Schurtz Smith (who later changed his name to Carl Schurtz Carlsmith) was a Hilo attorney and former judge, then serving a term as representative in the Territorial Legislature. His potential for political leadership was apparent when he attended Stanford University, where he was elected vice-president of the student body less than three weeks after admission.[30] Now, he served as legal advisor to President Jordan in the matter of Jane Stanford's death. Smith conferred with Dr. Waterhouse, dealt with financial expenses incurred by the estate, and discussed Stanford faculty salaries with the president.

Two assignments Jordan gave Smith were widely reported in the newspapers. First, he was to release to the press the Jordan and Hopkins statement affirming Mrs. Stanford's natural death, but only after the *Alameda*, bearing her coffin and the Stanford party, had slipped her lines. Then, he was to send a telegram to Mountford Wilson, and provide a statement to the Associated Press, to the effect that Miss Berner had taken the same dose of bicarbonate of soda and cascara at the same time as Mrs. Stanford without ill effect. Presumably this two-pronged approach to public disclosure was intended to keep Berner's name from appearing in the official statement.

At the last minute before sailing, Jordan called Mr. Kidd of the Associated Press from the wharf to cancel the telegram, or, if he had already sent it, to phone Smith and instruct him to deny the story. Undoubtedly confused, and acting with judicial caution, Smith requested Mr. Kidd to hand-deliver Jordan's message, which read: "Carl Smith. Kindly suppress cablegram. Not quite true. Jordan." Smith promptly dispatched a letter to Jordan informing him it had been too late to recall the cablegram.[31] Jordan answered that when Mr. Kidd informed him that he had heard differently from Miss Berner, "it seemed best to suppress the cablegram, but I regret that the suppression was not quite complete. It however makes no difference."[32] By then, Jordan had developed a different idea about the bicarbonate of soda.

Smith released the press statement, which appeared in the March 15 evening news in Honolulu and in mainland newspapers the next day. Issued jointly by Jordan and Hopkins, it paraphrased the Waterhouse report:

In our judgment, after careful consideration of all facts brought to our knowledge, we are fully convinced that Mrs. Stanford's death was not due to strychnine poisoning nor to intentional wrong-doing on the part of any one. We find in the statements of those with her in her last moments, no evidence that any of the characteristic symptoms of strychnine poisoning were present. We think it probable that her death was due to a combination of conditions and circumstances. Among these we may note, in connection with her advanced age, the unaccustomed exertion, a surfeit of unsuitable food and the unusual exposure on the picnic party of the day in question. . . . The occurrence of th[e] strychnine in the bicarbonate of soda is as yet unexplained. The fact that it is not in excess of usual medicinal proportions suggests either an error of a pharmacist or else that the combination was prepared for tonic purposes.

In drafting his statement, Jordan chose his words with care: "after ~~full~~ careful consideration," " . . . nor to ~~poisoning, evil,~~ intentional wrongdoing," and he deleted altogether the lines he had jotted down calling attention to the Poland water poisoning.[33]

The Attending Physicians' Response

The *Evening Bulletin* of March 15 also published a dockside interview with President Jordan. "Dr. Jordan stated," the interview began, "that Dr. Humphris, according to his opinion, knew little or nothing about strychnine poisoning and the other physicians took Humphris' statement of the case on which to base their conclusions. Dr. Jordan has gone into the details of the Stanford case very thoroughly and one of his last assertions in connection with the scientific side . . . was practically that Dr. Humphris and his associates don't know what they are talking about."

Leaving Honolulu before issuing his press release allowed Dr. Jordan to escape confrontation by the four physicians who were directly involved in Mrs. Stanford's case. As a result, they too felt compelled to issue a statement, and it was published as the lead article in the *Pacific Commercial Advertiser* on March 17, 1905. The statement strongly affirmed their conviction that Mrs. Stanford had died of strychnine poisoning. It reviewed the symptoms and utterances of her final moments, the salient necropsy findings and coroner's inquest testimony, and quoted passages on strychnine poisoning from the *Reference Handbook of Medical Science* (1904) and S. O. L. Potter's *Materia Medica, Pharmacy and Therapeutics*. The Honolulu physicians were in full agreement:

> She did not die of angina pectoris [this diagnosis was not given in the Jordan-Hopkins statement but could be inferred] because neither the symptoms of the attack nor the condition of the heart confirms that diagnosis.
>
> It is imbecile to think that a woman of Mrs. Stanford's age and known mental characteristics might have died of an hysterical seizure in half an hour.[34]
>
> "Her advanced age, the unaccustomed exertion, surfeit of unsuitable food and the unusual exposure", either separately or combined, could not cause death as Mrs. Stanford died.
>
> No Board of Health in existence could allow a certificate based on such a cause of death to go unchallenged.[35]

They said that they found the statement of Jordan and Hopkins "astonishing" and felt obliged to publish their report in order that it might receive the same publicity. Yet, aside from brief notices—"Henry still holds to poisoning theory," "Honolulu Doctors Dispute Jordan's Version"—and later publication by the *Call* of the full text of the Honolulu physicians' statement without comment, their angry rebuttal attracted little attention on the mainland. The *Palo Alto Times* put the matter to rest on the day of the funeral: "That the death of Mrs. Jane L. Stanford was due to natural causes has been proven beyond question."[36] Jordan's proclamation had indeed succeeded in quashing the contention that she had died of strychnine poisoning.

Studio portrait of Jane Lathrop Stanford, ca. 1904. Courtesy of the Stanford University Archives.

Bertha Berner, Mrs. Stanford's private secretary for twenty-one years, at the Stanford home in Palo Alto. Berner was an enigma to newsmen. Some thought her to be Belgian, others German. One columnist had her growing up in Oconomowoc, Wisconsin, another in Atchison, Kansas, where she was said to ask her childhood friends to call her "Ruby." Courtesy of the Stanford University Archives.

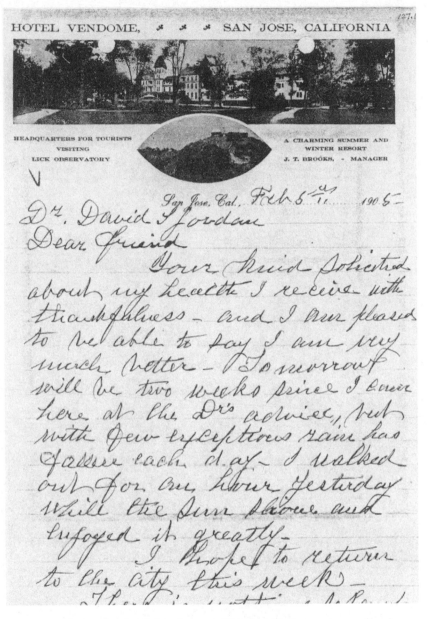

HOTEL VENDOME, ❋ ❋ ❋ SAN JOSE, CALIFORNIA

HEADQUARTERS FOR TOURISTS
VISITING
LICK OBSERVATORY

A CHARMING SUMMER AND
WINTER RESORT
J. T. BROOKS, - MANAGER

San Jose. Cal. Feb 5ᵗʰ 1905—

Dr. David S Jordan
Dear Friend
            Your kind Solicited
about my health I receive with
thankfulness — and I am pleased
to be able to say I am very
much better — Tomorrow
will be two weeks since I came
here at the Dr's advice, but
with few exceptions rain has
fallen each day — I walked
out for an hour yesterday
while the Sun shone and
enjoyed it greatly —
            I hope to return
to the city this week —

A portion of Mrs. Stanford's last letter to President Jordan, written a few days after she learned that the Poland water had contained a lethal dose of strychnine. She and Berner returned to the city the next day, stopping in Palo Alto to purchase bicarbonate of soda. Courtesy of the Stanford University Archives.

The last known photograph of Mrs. Stanford, said to have been taken by a friend on February 14, 1905, the day she sailed for Honolulu. Courtesy of the Stanford University Archives.

Nob Hill mansions of Mark Hopkins (*left*) and Leland Stanford, at the corner of Powell (*shown*) and California Streets. The pharmacy is not Wakelee's, to which Elizabeth Richmond, the maid, took the Poland water on the night of January 14, 1905, which was approximately the same distance away, but down California Street. Courtesy of the San Francisco History Center, San Francisco Public Library.

Mrs. Stanford posing at the Sphinx in January 1904 with three of the four leading suspects in her murder—Alfred Beverly, the butler, and Bertha Berner,
mounted, and Elizabeth Richmond, seated, on the camels. Courtesy of the Stanford University Archives.

EXTRA!

The Bulletin.

VOLUME 109 · 19th Year. · SAN FRANCISCO, WEDNESDAY EVENING, MARCH 1, 1905. · NUMBER 145

MRS. STANFORD DIES, POISONED

"I HAVE BEEN POISONED! THIS IS A TERRIBLE DEATH TO DIE"

WERE MRS. STANFORD'S LAST WORDS

HONOLULU, March 1.—Mrs. Jane Lathrop Stanford of San Francisco, widow of United States Senator Leland Stanford, died at 11:40 o'clock last night at the Moana Hotel here. Suspicious circumstances surround the death of Mrs. Stanford. She was taken ill at eleven o'clock, and said:

"I have been poisoned!" Her last words were: "This is a horrible death to die!"

The police are conducting an investigation.

FOUND ON FLOOR OF
HOTEL IN HONOLULU.
DEATH SOON FOLLOWS

BALFOUR IS STOESSEL IS

The Daily Palo Alto.

Special Edition

Vol. XXVI. STANFORD UNIVERSITY, CAL., WEDNESDAY, MARCH 1, 1905. No. 36.

MRS. STANFORD DIES
SUDDENLY IN HAWAII

End Came Unexpectedly to the Widow of the Senator and the Joint Founder of the University Last Night.

Jane Lathrop Stanford, one of the founders of the University, is dead. According to a telegram received this morning by Charles G. Lathrop, Mrs. Stanford passed away suddenly in Honolulu last night. The telegram came from the physician who has been attending Mrs. Stanford during the past few weeks, but beyond the brief warning of Mrs. Stanford's end, it contained no further information as to the cause.

Following is the text of the message received by Mr. Lathrop from Honolulu:

"HONOLULU, March 1.

"Mrs. Stanford died suddenly.   DR. HUMPHRIES, Moana Hotel, Honolulu."

TOP: Sensational headline of *The Bulletin*. Hasty reporting and typesetting may account for the errors and ambiguity. Mrs. Stanford's last words were, "This is a horrible death to die," according to Bertha Berner's sworn testimony. BOTTOM: Special edition of *The Daily Palo Alto* misinforming campus readers that Mrs. Stanford, said to be in her eightieth year, had been under the care of Dr. Humphries [*sic*] during the previous few weeks. The reporter concluded, "According to the best information obtainable, her death was due to terminal pneumonia."

Street-side photograph of the Moana Hotel, Waikiki, Hawaii, taken October 3, 1909. Mrs. Stanford's room, above the arch in the right wing, looked out on the trolley line, not the ocean. Courtesy of the Bishop Museum.

The royal palm driveway of Queen's Hospital, Honolulu, Hawaii, ca. 1908.
Mrs. Stanford's autopsy was performed in the morgue and was attended by
seven members of the Queen's medical staff. Courtesy of the Bishop Museum.

David Starr Jordan, president of Stanford University, ca. 1898. Courtesy of the Stanford University Archives.

Captain Jules Callundan (*right*) discusses a case in 1898 with Harry Morse at the Harry Morse Detective and Patrol Agency. From the private collection of John E. Boessenecker.

Dr. F. Howard Humphris, who attended Mrs. Stanford in her last moments of life. Courtesy of the Hawaii Medical Library.

Dr. Harry V. Murray, who arrived at Mrs. Stanford's room the moment she died. Courtesy of the Hawaii Medical Library.

TOP LEFT: Dr. Francis R. Day, who brought a stomach pump, but too late.
TOP RIGHT: Dr. Clifford B. Wood, who performed Mrs. Stanford's autopsy.
BOTTOM LEFT: Dr. Ernest C. Waterhouse, who served as consultant to
President Jordan. BOTTOM RIGHT: Dr. John S. B. Pratt, who took the
forensic evidence from the deputy sheriff. Photos courtesy of the Hawaii
Medical Library.

Dr. Edmund C. Shorey, who performed Mrs. Stanford's toxicological analyses. Courtesy of the Queen's University (Ontario) Archives.

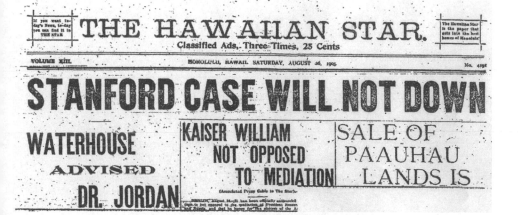

The *Hawaiian Star*'s scoop, "Waterhouse Advised Jordan," attracted little attention on the mainland.

Mrs. Stanford's Honolulu cortege proceeding to the SS *Alameda* on March 15, 1905. Courtesy of the Stanford University Archives.

SS *Alameda* in Honolulu Harbor, Oahu, Hawaii, ca. 1900. In her memoir, Bertha Berner claimed that Stanford officials had chartered the 100-cabin *Alameda*: "Only those of the funeral group were on the steamer going home. One end of the steamer contained a bier with the casket banked with floral tributes." Contemporary news accounts, however, placed Mrs. Stanford's casket in the hold and quoted Berner as having had pleasant conversations with the passengers on the voyage. Courtesy of the Bishop Museum.

P A R T T W O

6 ⌒ The Stanford Party Returns Home

Dr. Jordan and Captain Callundan Meet the Press

President Jordan returned to the Stanford University campus on the afternoon of Tuesday, March 21. That morning he had been surrounded by reporters as he disembarked from the *Alameda* in San Francisco. A columnist from the *San Francisco Call* summarized the interview:

"How do you account for the presence of the half grain of strychnine found in the bicarbonate of soda . . . ?" "That is a leading question" came the answer and President Jordan turned half around, indicating he was averse to saying anything further on this point.

"Are we to understand that you discredit the chemist, the doctors and the Honolulu officials?" Then President Jordan made a remark of startling import. His manner was of as much significance as his words: "I know all about them and their work." It may be inferred safely within the bounds of careful interpretation that President Jordan meant to convey the conviction in his mind that not all the doctors and chemists and officials connected with the investigation in Honolulu are at least trustworthy. "Do you mean to say that there was a conspiracy . . . to make it appear that Mrs. Stanford was poisoned when as a matter of fact they knew there was no evidence to support such a theory?" Dr. Jordan made no reply.

"Are we to believe that some one mixed the strychnine crystals in the bicarbonate of soda after Mrs. Stanford took the dose . . . to make it appear that she had been poisoned?" But the president was through with interviewing along this line.[1]

The dockside interview is remarkable in light of Jordan's later allegations of improper medical care, tampering with the bicarbonate of soda, fraudulent chemical analyses, and complex conspiracy. How prescient the journalist who scripted Jordan's subsequent actions in the case was!

On the same day, detectives Callundan and Reynolds reported to police headquarters, where they summarized the results of their investigations in Honolulu for Acting Chief Spillane and Captain Burnett. The full report was to have been delivered to Mountford Wilson, but no copy of it has survived; it was probably lost in the April 1906 San Francisco earthquake and fire, along with the police and Morse agency files. What the investigation disclosed is known only through newspaper accounts of the meeting of March 21, 1905. Undoubtedly, there were many details that were not touched upon, but the press covered several main points, and it is possible to form an opinion of the quality of the Honolulu investigation.

In its March 22, 1905, issue, the *Call* reported that when the detectives interviewed the same witnesses who had testified at the inquest, they discovered inconsistencies that disproved the poisoning diagnosis. Captain Callundan had closely questioned Dr. Humphris about the symptoms and signs of strychnine poisoning and had come away from the interview with serious doubts about the physician's diagnostic acumen.[2] Miss Berner had also given Callundan new details of the death scene that he could not reconcile with a diagnosis of strychnine poisoning. The key new information was that Mrs. Stanford died seated in a chair, "instead of dying in her bed as he [Humphris] had previously asserted." Moreover, if she died in a chair, "the convulsions that invariably attend the dying moments of a victim of strychnine poisoning [would be] so severe that it would be impossible to even hold a patient on a chair."

She could not have had such convulsions, the report said, as neither the pan of water in her lap nor the bucket of water on the floor, in which her limbs were bathed, was upset. How, if a convulsion had been in progress, could she have reached for Berner's hands and placed them on her cheeks at the very moment of death? "Considerable importance is attached to this proved fact," the journalist wrote. DIED IN CHAIR, the column emphasized.

Other evidence suggesting that Mrs. Stanford had died of natural causes came to light during Callundan's further interrogation of Berner. There appeared to have been an "overindulgence in exercise" on the picnic outing, as well as a remarkable gorging on food by Mrs. Stanford, if Berner were to be believed: four Swiss cheese sandwiches, two tongue sandwiches, two lettuce sandwiches, two or three large pieces of gingerbread, two cups of cold coffee, and twelve or fourteen pieces of French candy. The amount of food consumed by Mrs. Stanford "should have entered into the considerations of the autopsy surgeons," declared Callundan. STOMACH HURTS HEART, the column read.

"These facts, revealed by the persistent inquiry of Captain Callundan," the *Call* reporter concluded, "readily appealed to President Jordan and were responsible for his conclusions that Mrs. Stanford was not poisoned." The "facts," as reported, warrant closer examination.

In addition to his misrepresentation of Dr. Humphris's inquest testimony (both Humphris and Murray had clearly indicated that Mrs. Stanford died in a chair), Callundan appears to have had a seriously restricted concept of a strychnine-induced tetanic *spasm*. He pictured the event as one in which a *convulsion* wracked the body, the limbs and body jerked uncontrollably, water basins were overturned, and the patient was thrown to the floor. To the detective, Humphris's apparent ignorance of such a characteristic convulsive syndrome cast doubt on his diagnostic capabilities.

A typical grand mal epileptic seizure, as many readers will know, has two clinical phases: the first is a "tonic" phase, in which there is involuntary *sustained* contraction of the muscles; the second is a "clonic" phase, in which there is *repetitive* contraction and relaxation of muscles, resulting in convulsive jerking. Hence, the episode is often designated a "tonic-clonic seizure." The first phase consists of a tetanic *spasm*, the second of a *convulsion*. Mrs. Stanford's terminal event was a tetanic spasm, the characteristic result of strychnine-induced disinhibition of motoneurons of the spinal cord. One can attribute Callundan's insistence that Mrs. Stanford had experienced a convulsion to his medical naïveté. Jordan's is explained less easily.

Were the reports of too much exercise and food evidentiary? On March 14, Bertha Berner wrote to Dr. Waterhouse that Mrs. Stanford had sat on a carriage cushion throughout lunch in the picnic grove. At departure time, she had had to be helped to her feet, and she then walked slowly for a few minutes "for the purpose . . . of getting her blood into circulation."[3] Even though on the way home, the party stopped briefly at the Royal Mausoleum and the Sachs store, an "overindulgence in exercise" is an extravagant conclusion in light of testimony that two days earlier Mrs. Stanford had enjoyed a brisk late-afternoon walk lasting more than one hour.

The sandwiches put up by the Moana Hotel had been described by the *Pacific Commercial Advertiser* reporter as tongue, cheese, and lettuce between two pieces of bread. Surely Mrs. Stanford did not disassemble the meat and cheese sandwiches to make new ones out of each ingredient individually. As to the amount of food she ate, at autopsy, her stomach contained only the water drunk just before death, and it was not distended.

Dr. Jordan's Strychnine Theory

Back in his office on March 22, Dr. Jordan dictated the first of several letters to address how strychnine had gotten into the bicarbonate of soda. Attributing the poison's presence to deliberate compounding or pharmacist's error, as had been done in his press release, became less plausible in light of a widely featured interview with the pharmacist, W. E. Jackson of the Stanford Pharmacy in Palo Alto. Mr. Jackson said he had sold three ounces of bicarbonate of soda to Mrs. Stanford and Miss Berner on February 6, 1905; it did not contain strychnine, either by prescription or by accident.[4]

Jordan may not have been aware of Jackson's disclosure when he drafted his press release. That it came to his attention is suggested by the wording of his March 22 letter to Judge Samuel F. Leib, successor to Mrs. Stanford as president of the Stanford University Board of Trustees: "If the tonic theory of strychnine is not acceptable, you have the other, that it was put in by the doctor to bolster up his case, after he had had time to read up the symptoms a little . . . [he is] a man without professional or personal standing."[5] Humphris bolstered up his case "by having the bottle made to correspond with his diagnosis," Jordan wrote to the attorney Mountford Wilson on the same day, requesting that the executor refresh Mr. Callundan's memory on that point.[6]

One can imagine Wilson's confusion: first a cablegram attesting to the benignity of the bicarbonate of soda, which had caused no ill effects when Berner took it; then a retraction of that claim when Mr. Kidd of the Associated Press said that it was not true;[7] then a press release suggesting that strychnine had been present as the result of a pharmacist's error; and, finally, the extraordinary idea that Dr. Humphris had himself laced the bicarbonate of soda with strychnine.

Jordan's letter to Wilson the following day may well have heightened the confusion. He told of learning from Mrs. Lathrop that Mrs. Stanford had taken a dose of soda while recuperating at the Hotel

Vendome, had found it stale, and had purchased a new supply in Palo Alto (in agreement with the druggist Jackson's account). "I am coming to be more and more convinced that the bottle was tampered with on the night of Mrs. Stanford's death," Jordan wrote, evidently dismissing from his thinking the testimony of Berner and Hunt that the bottle had sat accessible to all in a room of Mrs. Stanford's San Francisco mansion for nearly a week.[8] By March 24, the day of Mrs. Stanford's funeral, Jordan had become "morally certain," that strychnine had been put into the bottle of bicarbonate of soda after Mrs. Stanford's death. His advice to Judge Carl Smith in Honolulu was to "keep watch of the actions as well as of the past history of the two physicians at the Moana Hotel."[9]

Dr. Humphris's Pique

Within a day or two, Jordan received letters from Judge Smith and Dr. Humphris. Each enclosed the clipping from the *Bulletin* featuring the derogatory remarks Jordan had allegedly made against Dr. Humphris. Smith expressed confidence that Jordan had not given the statement, but "wonder[ed] how it found its way into the paper."[10] Humphris was succinct: "Will you kindly say whether it is true that you made this statement?"[11] Humphris prided himself on his scientific approach to medical practice, and the implication in the clipping that he was deficient in the "scientific side" must have made him bristle. One cannot but wonder if libel was on the mind of each writer. Jordan responded to both men that he had no recollection of saying anything resembling the remarks the reporter had attributed to him. To Humphris, he added that his conclusion that Mrs. Stanford had not died of strychnine poisoning was "based on very careful cross-examination of Miss Berner and Miss Hunt by one of the best informed physicians of Honolulu, and on the judgment of various others."[12]

"I felt sure that you could not have expressed the sentiment attributed to you," Humphris began his smooth rejoinder, and he continued in a tone that suggested that the matter was far from over:

The other doctors and I engaged in the case feel however that our judgement having been called in question "by one of the best informed physicians of Honolulu" we are justified in asking the name of this gentleman, as, in the interests of science apart from this particular case, we would wish to discuss with him upon what grounds he differs from us.

The case is an interesting one and if it can be shown scientifically that the four Doctors erred, let it be so shown. We all therefore will feel obliged if you will kindly favor us with the name.[13]

Jordan did not answer this letter. It would not be until the following year that he would hear from Humphris again.

Dr. Shorey's Position

Dr. Edmund Shorey may have gotten wind of Jordan's suspicions of a medical conspiracy, because he soon wrote to him to clarify his position. He had nothing to do with the statement of the Honolulu physicians, he assured Jordan. His role had been strictly that of an analytical chemist, and, as he thought he had made clear in his testimony, "the chemical facts in the case do not warrant *any* opinion as to how Mrs. Stanford came to her death."[14] He was prompted to write to preserve his professional reputation. He had worked diligently to recover strychnine from Mrs. Stanford's organs, but he had found only a positive fading purple test, an indication insufficient for him to incriminate strychnine.

Jordan answered that he had been surprised when he saw Dr. Shorey's name added to the statement of the physicians, because "Mr. Callundan . . . left me with an extremely favorable impression of your skill as a chemist and of your justice as a man."[15] Jordan's opinion of Shorey would change sharply two years later.

Perhaps feeling the need of a professional ally in Honolulu, Jordan shared new medical and investigative details with the toxicologist. One guesses that they were of little interest to Shorey, who focused more on organic chemistry than medical controversies. From "cross-examination" of the women, Jordan wrote, it was evident that "there was no strychnine spasm or anything approaching it; that Mrs. Stanford died sitting in an ordinary small chair without arms, holding the vessel in her lap," which differed from the other accounts.[16] Mrs. Stanford, Jordan also revealed, had suffered from a congenital (and hereditary) "distortion" of one of her limbs, which was well known to her closest friends, a point of medical history that, if shared with Waterhouse, never factored into the consultant's thinking.[17]

Regardless of the cordial exchange and novel disclosures, despite Shorey's clear lack of support of the poisoning diagnosis and Callundan's measure of his integrity, the chemist, too, became a figure in Jordan's conspiracy theory when the president began to wonder whether the bicarbonate of soda had *ever* contained strychnine.

Jordan copied this correspondence to Mountford Wilson and kept him apprised of other developments in Honolulu. One that was particularly irksome to Jordan (and was surely factored into his conspiracy theory) was the hefty bill submitted by the deputy sheriff for the lengthy transcripts his clerks, Sea and Van Gieson, had typed—60¢ per page, 30¢ per first carbon. Jordan asked Smith to see what he could do. Smith discovered that this was the standard court stenographers' fee set by the U.S. District Court for the Territory of Hawaii. He reported that he was unable to persuade the stenographers "to take the view of the matter which we do" and paid the bill.[18]

Dr. Waterhouse Confronted

On March 31, 1905, Dr. Waterhouse submitted a bill for his professional fee to Carl Smith, who forwarded it to Jordan with his approval. The fee of $350 was based on time and energy, Smith said emphatically, not on any other consideration. In forwarding the bill to Mountford Wilson in his capacity as executor of Mrs. Stanford's estate, Jordan reassured him of Carl Smith's judgment that Dr. Waterhouse was "the best informed physician in Honolulu,"[19] that he had spent an afternoon interviewing Berner and Hunt to secure a more accurate account "than was obtained from any other source, and . . . gave us the all important assurance that under no circumstances could Mrs. Stanford's death have been due to poisoning." In rendering this service, Dr. Waterhouse had given up his practice for three or four days, Jordan exaggerated, while also reminding Wilson that "the scale of fees is very much higher in Honolulu than on the mainland."[20]

The thorny issue of the consultant arose again, brought to Jordan's attention by both Smith and Waterhouse.[21] Dr. Humphris had shown Dr. Day the letter from Jordan in which he denied the disparaging comments attributed to him by the *Evening Bulletin* and spoke of the cross-examination of Mrs. Stanford's attendants by "one of the best informed physicians of Honolulu," without revealing his name. Day, recalling that he had seen Waterhouse dining with Jordan at the University Club, "put two and two together [so Waterhouse deduced]," and he and Humphris confronted their colleague. Day accused Waterhouse of unprofessional conduct; Humphris asked for a copy of his report.

Waterhouse immediately sought the advice of Judge Smith, who informed him that, inasmuch as he had been "substantially" paid, the report was now the private property of Dr. Jordan. Smith admonished Waterhouse not to release it.

"There could be no case in the world of greater importance than this," Jordan wrote to reassure Waterhouse. The accusations of his colleagues were totally unjustified, and his report was in the hands of the executors, who would not even consider releasing it to Humphris without a formal petition. Jordan told Waterhouse that in response to an inquiry by Humphris, he had revealed the consultant's identity, as well as Captain Callundan's employment of Dr. William E. Taylor as an expert witness.[22] Taylor, it will be recalled, was the senior physician at the autopsy, but had been present at only part of it. If he rendered an opinion, it was never revealed to the public, and his role in the matter was never reported in the newspapers (he died in 1906). More important, Jordan had not revealed the names of Waterhouse and Taylor to Dr. Humphris as he claimed. He did eventually disclose Waterhouse's consultancy, but not until long after the Honolulu newspapers had revealed it to the public.

In his April 15 letter to Jordan, Smith predicted "a call from Dr. Humphris in this matter but inasmuch as I have had several years of experience in dealing with men of his sort, I do not anticipate any difficulties in the interview." Anticipations notwithstanding, the matter did heat up, leading Smith shortly to write again. Jordan summarized the situation for Wilson by quoting two paragraphs from Smith's letter:

Dr. Waterhouse has just left for Ceylon. Before leaving, Dr. Day threatened him with an attack in the medical journals, and Dr. Humphris backs up the threat with others. Both Day and Humphris tried to coerce Waterhouse into a signed statement by which he would retract from some of his conclusions. At my suggestion, he remains perfectly quiet on the matter.

Humphris and the rest are now spreading the story that you, with your training as a physician twenty-five years ago, are trying to discredit up-to-date and well equipped men.[23]

We do not know whether Waterhouse headed to Ceylon to escape the threats of exposure by his colleagues or if his trip had long been planned for the purpose of exploring agricultural opportunities in the Far East. He had a strong interest in cultivating rubber trees. He grew saplings in containers in his back yard, and a few months earlier he had persuaded his brother-in-law, George Harding, to travel to Pahang, Malaya to look over plantation prospects. It seems reasonable to suppose that his sizable fee from Stanford facilitated his Far Eastern enterprise.[24] When he returned to Honolulu three months later, however, charges of unethical conduct awaited him.

7 ⌒ Bolstering Dr. Jordan's Diagnosis

No Poison Found

The Honolulu police department did not investigate the case further, having concluded that the poison had originated in San Francisco. High Sheriff Henry was quoted as saying, "We have done our duty, proving that murder was done. It is now up to the San Francisco police to get the murderer."[1] In fact, although there was considerable criticism of the Honolulu police department over what was perceived to be a slipshod and superficial crime investigation, the coroner's inquest had accomplished precisely what the law required—identifying the deceased and determining when, where, and by what means she had come to her death. Eyewitnesses, attending physicians, autopsy findings, and toxicological analyses were all that were required. It is when the coroner's jury determines that there has been foul play that a full police investigation is triggered, and the Honolulu authorities had acted correctly in referring the case to San Francisco.

Whether or not the results of the detectives' investigation satisfied Acting Police Chief John Spillane is not known, but the San Francisco police department also closed the case. It was an unsettled time for the department. By the end of March 1905, Spillane, who had been in office for only a few weeks, following the dismissal of Chief George Wittman, was replaced by Detective Sergeant Jeremiah Dinan. The new chief, backed by Boss Ruef and Mayor Schmitz, was promoted to the position over seven police captains. Only three weeks earlier, Dinan had been working on the Stanford case, sweating witnesses and searching the mansion for strychnine. Chief Dinan would have been easily persuaded that no further investigation was wanted.[2]

It was police inaction in the case that spurred Welton Stanford, a nephew of Leland Stanford, to place a notice in the *San Francisco Examiner* on May 25, 1905, offering a reward of $1,000 to find and convict the killer of his aunt. He had read the coroner's inquest and autopsy reports, and he was convinced that she had been murdered. He was distressed by the lack of progress in the investigation. Could it then have been only coincidence when the *Examiner* published a column the following day under the banner "No Poison in Body of Founder" and suggested that Mr. Stanford's inducements were not necessary? The report, issued by the executors of the Stanford estate, claimed that Mrs. Stanford's internal organs had undergone thorough study in the chemistry laboratories of the university, with negative results. "It bears out the theory first advanced by President David Starr Jordan. . . . There will be no further use now for private detectives. . . . The case from that standpoint is closed."[3]

The *Pacific Commercial Advertiser* ran the story a week later. The reactions of the physicians, and particularly of Duncan and Shorey, can only be guessed at, but incredulity must have been foremost. To which internal organs did the *San Francisco Examiner* article refer? The organs in which strychnine would concentrate had been removed from Mrs. Stanford's body at autopsy and turned over to the chemists for analysis. They had been chopped, boiled, and reduced to a slurry that could not possibly be considered an internal organ. Any poisonous alkaloid that might have been in the original tissues had been thoroughly shaken out with chloroform and dried to the residue giving the fading-purple color test. At best, the Stanford party left Honolulu with Mrs. Stanford's brain and heart in separate jars. Nothing further was ever heard of the brain, and the heart was said to have been delivered to Dr. William Ophüls, head of pathology at the Cooper Medical College in San Francisco.

The Ophüls Report

The *San Francisco Examiner* article was the first of the stories about the reexamination of Mrs. Stanford's remains, a supposed fresh look at her organs that eventually acquired the stature of a second autopsy. The *New York Times* attributed to Dr. Jordan the statement, "a postmortem examination showed that the aorta had been ruptured . . . as the result of fatty degeneration of the heart. The heart is now in San Francisco where it is being preserved."[4] The "autopsy" by Dr. Ophüls had proved "some form of heart lesion," Jordan told the Stanford trustees.

Bertha Berner also refers to what has now become known as the Ophüls report. In her popular and widely quoted memoir, *Mrs. Leland Stanford: An Intimate Account*, published by the Stanford University Press in 1935, Berner writes, "Mr. Hopkins ordered the vital organs and body fluids conveyed to San Francisco for further investigation," and she quotes the major conclusion of the Ophüls report:

None of the symptoms observed before her death are incompatible with the assumption that she died of heart disease, in fact they are best explained by this diagnosis. It is our opinion, therefore, based upon the previous history of the deceased, that the most probable cause of the death of Mrs. Stanford was chronic myocarditis [chronic disease of the heart muscles resulting from partial obstruction of the blood vessels of the heart].[5]

But it bears notice that Berner also wrote about her life with Mrs. Stanford in an earlier version of her memoir, published in 1934 by Edwards Brothers, Ann Arbor, Michigan, under the title *Incidents in the Life of Mrs. Leland Stanford by Her Private Secretary, Bertha Berner*. The Stanford University Press apparently bought the rights, gave the book a new title, and reissued it with changes the following year. The account about the reexamination of Mrs. Stanford's organs differs in Berner's earlier version: "Mr. Hopkins ordered the vital organs and body fluids conveyed to San Francisco for further investigation, *and after the examination of these organs, and several conferences of the physicians engaged in the matter, the decision arrived at by a group of surgeons of the Cooper Medical College was that death was due to a rupture of the coronary artery, shown by an examination of the heart* [italics added]."[6]

In addition to deleting the italicized clause in the Stanford University Press edition (thereby eliminating the diagnosis that Jordan favored, "rupture of the coronary artery"), Miss Berner quotes the Ophüls report with a slight but very significant difference. In the Edwards Brothers' edition, the clause about partial obstruction of the blood vessels is in parentheses, not brackets. In the Stanford University Press edition, the clause is in brackets, suggesting that either Miss Berner or her editor regarded it as an emendation to the Ophüls report, not a conclusion of the report itself. If such were the case, the pathologist's diagnosis was simply "chronic myocarditis." The parentheses reappeared in G. W. Nagel's 1975 book *Jane Stanford: Her Life and Letters*.[7] John

Boessenecker's 1998 *Lawman: The Life and Times of Harry Morse* substitutes an em dash.[8]

"Chronic myocarditis," a term then in vogue in medical texts, did not usually signify inflammation of the heart muscle, as the reader might infer from the "-itis," but referred to patchy areas of myocardial fibrosis or scarring, sometimes accompanied by fatty infiltration of the heart in obese persons. These were the "whitish opaque areas" and "fatty infiltration of the muscle" Dr. Wood had noted in his autopsy report. Both myocardial fibrosis and coronary arteriosclerosis were common in the elderly, but in the absence of symptoms of angina pectoris, the significance of the scarred areas was uncertain, owing to "a want of uniformity or constancy in the relation of these to the symptoms," as the cardiologist Robert H. Babcock states the dilemma. Babcock continues, "in dealing with this phase of cardiac disease one is at a loss whether to attempt to consider it from the standpoint of the pathologist or the clinician. In either case one is pretty sure to get himself into trouble."[9]

Dr. William Ophüls (the first dean of Stanford Medical School), who had a strong interest and record of investigation in cardiovascular disease, found in his unselected autopsy series that 100 percent of women had moderate to severe arteriosclerosis by the age of 60. About chronic myocarditis, Ophüls writes: "There are also cases in which one finds scars without any gross or microscopic lesions in the coronary arteries. Such scars, no doubt, result from healed true myocarditis. I believe that this occurs more commonly than is generally acknowledged."[10] Ophüls cautions: "The functional importance of the more localized myocardial lesions has not been finally determined."[11] Reading the original Ophüls report on Mrs. Stanford's heart might be clarifying, but, unfortunately, it has never been found. The genesis of Berner's versions of the report is not known.

Dr. Waterhouse Exposed

During the summer of 1905, the San Francisco newspapers carried little about Mrs. Stanford's death but instead engaged in a frenzy of reporting on President Jordan's firing of Professor Julius Goebel, chairman of the German Department, a confidant of Mrs. Stanford's and an outspoken critic of the president. The charges against Goebel were not of an academic nature; they alluded to interpersonal relations and, of all things, his failure properly to check out and return library books. The striking conjunction of dates relating to Mrs. Stanford's death and Professor Goebel's dismissal has been revealed by the recent research of W. B. Carnochan, a Stanford University professor of English.[12]

In late August 1905, however, in the midst of the Goebel uproar, a brief story appeared in the *Call* to the effect that there had been attempts by Stanford representatives to induce the four Honolulu physicians to reconsider their diagnosis of strychnine poisoning. On August 23, 1905, a columnist for the *Hawaiian Star* reported rumors that Timothy Hopkins had interviewed each physician when in Honolulu to retrieve Mrs. Stanford's body and intimated that the size of their fees might be overlooked in the event they dropped the diagnosis of strychnine poisoning.

"The doctors' reports apparently had not satisfied the wiseacres of the Stanford estate who had decided, many thousand miles away, that Mrs. Stanford had died of natural causes," wrote the reporter, who then grew frustrated when the physicians would not violate an ethical code to discuss the case with him and confirm the rumor of a bribe.[13] The columnist also disclosed that Dr. Wood had not been paid for his autopsy services, the Stanford estate contending that the autopsy was the responsibility of the territorial government. The bills of the other physicians, $150 each, had been paid. Mountford Wilson found the story undeserving of a denial; Callundan called it a lie. In an interview published in the September 4 issue of the *Hawaiian Star*, Humphris retorted, "Captain Callundan was not present at any of the interviews and cannot know what took place. He is simply entirely ignorant on the point."

The reporter continued to probe, nevertheless, and on August 26, 1905, the *Star* headlined a story under the banner, "Stanford Case Will Not Down: Waterhouse Advised Jordan. The President of Stanford University Still Discussing the Mysterious Moana Hotel Tragedy—His Opinion and That of Timothy Hopkins Based on Findings of a Doctor Who Never Saw the Deceased." The reporter presumably learned about Waterhouse's consultation from Day or Humphris, who may have delayed releasing the story until Waterhouse returned from Ceylon, as he had just a few days earlier. The paper reported that Waterhouse admitted his "lack of opportunities of direct observation seriously affected the value of his opinion."

Although the news was sensational in Honolulu (displacing columns on Kaiser Wilhelm's acceptance of President Teddy Roosevelt's mediation to end the Russo-Japanese War), it received little notice in San Francisco. There was no reason why it should have. Jordan had never disclosed Waterhouse's report, and the latter's name was not known in San Francisco. Jordan first drew on the Waterhouse report as proof of Mrs. Stanford's mode of natural death when he mentioned it in a letter to the Stanford trustees in September 1906. He brought it up again in the account he wrote for Stanford President Ray Lyman Wilbur and in his autobiography. Even descendants of Dr. Waterhouse were unaware of their ancestor's role in the Stanford mystery until they read about it in an article in the *Stanford Observer* published in 1991.[14]

A column in the *Call*, buried on page nine, reported that Waterhouse was the "only medical man in Honolulu who . . . would express an opinion in accordance with the views held by Dr. Jordan,"[15] and raised questions about Waterhouse's professional ethics. The *Call* also reported that Timothy Hopkins had "ocular proof" of Mrs. Stanford's tetanic spasm, having been sent a sketch of the diagnostic foot posture found at her autopsy. If the story is true, the deformation apparently failed to impress him. An editor in Honolulu put the issue in the broadest perspective when he wrote that knowledgeable physicians all over the country accepted strychnine poisoning as the correct diagnosis. At the time of these revelations, Dr. Jordan was out of the country, and there is no evidence that he offered a rebuttal.

Dr. Jordan's Conspiracy Theory

On December 31, 1905, the wire services in Denver, Colorado, dispatched a dramatic story claiming that Jordan, who was in Denver at the time, had accused Mrs. Stanford's servants of conspiring to jeopardize Berner's inheritance by poisoning the Poland water. He also accused the Honolulu officials, so the report said, of conspiring to extort large fees from Mrs. Stanford's estate by falsely declaring she had been murdered. The two branches of the conspiracy—servants and officials—clearly intertwined in his thinking. He promised a full and sensational report of his own investigation within a few weeks.

On his return to campus two days later, Dr. Jordan released a statement that the report from Denver was "a jumble of blunders, for which I take no responsibility," that he had only authorized the interviewer to communicate that "we were sure that Mrs. Stanford's death was due to natural causes."[16] Yet it is known that Jordan developed the complex conspiracy theory as early as April 1905, when he wrote to Professor Keinosuke Otaki in Tokyo about the false reports that Mrs. Stanford had died of strychnine poisoning, "the motive being apparently that a much larger fee would be possible in connection with a murder case than could be asked for a simple case of heart disease." Jordan also told Otaki that the Poland water had been poisoned "by one of the servants to spite some other one."[17]

The Denver interview was carried in the *Pacific Commercial Advertiser* and shared with High Sheriff Henry, who put Jordan's claim in a different light. Calling Jordan a "Science crank," Henry asserted that during his investigation he had learned that Stanford University was close to bankruptcy, that "the real purpose they [Jordan and Hopkins] were working for was to make it believed that Mrs. Stanford died from natural causes and was not murdered. I myself told them right to their faces that that was what they were trying to do."[18] Henry presumably assumed that they were trying to prevent lengthy delays in the probate of Mrs. Stanford's will, unaware that her bequest to the university was not particularly large. Or, more practically, he may have thought that Stanford simply hoped to save a few dollars in fees. An editorial poked fun at Henry's theory, and, one imagines, at Jordan's as well, referring to the university's $30 million endowment: the real conspiracy was hatched by rival university presidents threatened by Mrs. Stanford's inspirational work.[19]

It was on the basis of the Denver dispatch that the *New York Times* had quoted Jordan as stating that Mrs. Stanford died of a ruptured aorta. This diagnosis did not escape the attention of Dr. Humphris, who wrote directly in his telegraphic and arguably mischievous style: "I see by the papers that you have stated that the cause of Mrs. Stanford's death was rupture of the Aorta. Would you please let me know whether you said so, and if so what induced you to come to this conclusion."[20] Jordan replied that he had never claimed such a diagnosis, that he had merely said, "her death was due to [a] heart lesion of some form."[21]

Humphris was not easily dismissed. He pressured Jordan with ill-disguised disdain: "Many thanks for your prompt reply to my letter, if you could add to your courtesy by telling me why you think that Mrs. Stanford died from [a] heart lesion I should be very much obliged."[22]

Jordan responded with a full explanation—the examination of evidence by an expert panel of physicians, the insignificant traces of strychnine found by Dr. Shorey, the congenital deformity of her limb noted by Wood, the Waterhouse report (now safely revealed), all contributed to his thinking. He denied responsibility for the "foolish statements telegraphed from Denver." He had refrained from discussing the report of the pathological examination of the heart because he had not seen it, and it had not been published. He closed with a conjecture: "So far as I know, there is no clue to the incident of the Poland water. It certainly looks like a case of attempted poisoning, and it may be, of course, that the soda was vitiated by the same hand."[23]

This regression is remarkable in light of Dr. Jordan's previous assertions about the poisoning episodes, namely, that, in each instance, strychnine was added after the fact, and by Dr. Humphris himself in the case of the soda. Jordan's letter also informs us that the Ophüls report had not been published and that he was unaware of its conclusions (by then a year had elapsed since Mrs. Stanford's death). If intended to mollify Humphris, the explanations succeeded to the extent that he did not write again. But did they also signify an uncertainty in Jordan's mind about Mrs. Stanford's cause of death?

The Denver interview was covered fully by *San Francisco Call* reporters, who promptly questioned Captain Callundan, among others. The detective's responses, if reported factually, provide the only additional information available on the investigations carried out by the Harry Morse Detective and Patrol Agency. Callundan thought the Denver reporter must have misinterpreted Jordan's remarks, that the president could not have said the things the reporter claimed. Callundan explained that long ago he had cleared the servants of any role in Mrs. Stanford's poisoning; the Honolulu officials and physicians had worked hard and in good faith; all bills were appropriate and had been paid; and proof of Mrs. Stanford's death by heart disease had been found the previous May.

"It seems strange that Dr. Jordan should mention this again, for it was settled so long ago as to have almost entirely slipped the minds of all of us connected with the case," mused Callundan. He was emphatic that only he, Mountford Wilson, and Charles Lathrop knew the content of the report he had submitted months earlier, adding that it contained "nothing that would interest the public." As to the maid, Elizabeth Richmond, whom Jordan had implicated in the conspiracy against Berner, Captain Callundan was explicit: he thought her entirely innocent and had allowed her to return to England several months earlier.[24]

Whether new information about Richmond came to light is not known; it seems unlikely if she had returned to England. Much later, in his letter to President Wilbur in 1921, Jordan held her responsible for the Poland water poisoning. He said he was passing on the findings of Captain Callundan, who told him during a casual encounter in Placerville that the temporary maid, Elizabeth Richmond, had spiked the water with strychnine in an "insane freak," in one of her periodic attacks of mania. Callundan learned this, Dr. Jordan explained, from interviews of servants who told of Richmond's regaling them with tales of poisoning in the aristocratic English households where she had been employed.[25]

The problem was that the detective could not prove the charges. Nor could President Wilbur verify Jordan's claim, had he wished to, because Jules Callundan had died ten years earlier. The account did not jibe with the interview Callundan had given the *San Francisco Call*. As well, in describing Elizabeth Richmond as a "maid temporarily employed," Dr. Jordan seemed to have forgotten that she had been Mrs. Stanford's personal maid on travels half way around the world and back in 1903–4.

Dr. Jordan never released the report that the Denver interviewer had promised. Surprise may have been the reaction of some members of the Board of Trustees of Stanford University when President Jordan brought the matter up again, writing to them on September 24, 1906, to request their publication of the report of the "council of physicians and other reports necessary to show to the public the fact that the death of Mrs. Stanford was not due to strychnine poisoning."[26] He noted that the only statement ever given the public had been his and Mr. Hopkins's press release of March 1905. He was concerned over truth, justice, and clearing Miss Berner's name. What brought Jordan's concern to mind now, eighteen months after Mrs. Stanford's death, is unknown, but in any event the board did not act on his request.

Reports of the investigation of Mrs. Stanford's death had gone to Mountford Wilson, whose files were destroyed in the San Francisco fire following the earthquake that spring. One might wonder whether the board was likely to possess confidential medical files about Mrs. Stanford. Even if it had, as the Stanford English Professor Edith Mirrielees observes about another matter, "the trustees, living up to the 'trust' part of their title, let nothing escape that could be kept under cover."[27]

8   ⌒   The Cases of Shorey and Humphris

Jared Smith's Charges

Mrs. Stanford's case was kept alive for Dr. Jordan, long after most citizens had dismissed it from their curiosity, by a letter marked personal from Jared G. Smith, special agent in charge of the Hawaii Agricultural Experiment Station (see Appendix 1). The letter, dated December 27, 1906, began, "For your own information" and ended, "This matter has not been given wide publicity. . . ."[1] It gave shocking information about Edmund Shorey.

Dr. Shorey, the principal toxicologist in Mrs. Stanford's case, had begun employment at the Hawaii Agricultural Experiment Station in the fall of 1903. Sometime over the next three years, Smith and Shorey must have had a falling out. In November 1905, Smith had written to Jordan to ask if the president might arrange a Stanford degree for Frederick G. Krauss.[2] Mr. Krauss had entered the university in the pioneer class but had left in 1893 without a diploma. He was employed as an instructor at the Kamehameha Schools, and Smith engaged him part-time to conduct experiments in growing rice. Krauss's work so impressed Smith that he wanted to hire him at the station, but the post required a university degree. He wondered whether the work on rice could be given two years' credit at Stanford. Whether Jordan petitioned the Department of Agriculture is not known, but Krauss, like the entomologist Van Dine, was hired at the station without having been granted a Stanford degree. The main point of this digression is that in the fall of 1905 Jared Smith did not rail against Dr. Shorey.

Smith did not mince his words, however, when he wrote confidentially in December 1906. He said Van Dine had told him how much Jordan mistrusted Shorey in his dealings with him at the time of Mrs.

Stanford's death. He wanted Jordan to know that the chemist had been dismissed for "having written a series of venomous, libelous and vile anonymous letters."[3] Dr. Jordan answered that he had never met Shorey, had no reason to doubt the accuracy of his analyses of strychnine, and that the toxicologist had assured him that "he had not allied himself with the physicians who made such a bad break in Mrs. Stanford's case." Jordan added mysteriously that Smith's news "may throw light on certain other matters."[4]

Smith wrote back promptly, warning Jordan not to believe anything Shorey said: "he has been known to report one way officially and dramatically opposite for a fee in the same case." He claimed to know that Shorey had changed his position in the Stanford case (to what he did not say) and had not shared his fee with Mr. Duncan. "I believe," Smith closed, "he would sell his work or his reputation or whatever traces of an immortal soul there may be in him, to the highest bidder, or to any bidder, if he could cover up his trail. As to honor, he has none, absolutely."[5]

Dr. Shorey Accused of Fraud

Dr. Jordan thanked Smith for the information, intrigued that it seemed "to throw doubt as to whether any strychnine really existed in the carbonate of soda taken from Mrs. Stanford's room." That doubt did not exonerate Humphris as one might suppose; rather it drew Shorey into the conspiracy. "It was proved at Honolulu that the physician in question urged Dr. Shorey 'for God's sake to find strychnine in that bottle,' and he was able to find a trace of it."[6] Why, one might ask, had this supposed exchange between Humphris and Shorey not surfaced earlier, neither brought up in Jordan's gracious letter to Shorey nearly two years earlier, nor recalled in Jordan's letter to Smith one month earlier, when he did not doubt the accuracy of Shorey's work? Now, Jordan inquired if Mr. Smith might discuss with Mr. Duncan whether Shorey's report was, in fact, fraudulent. It is not known whether Smith posed the question to Duncan. What is known is that Duncan had also certified the analyses under oath, and he had held up a watch glass containing strychnine crystals for the coroner's jury to see. As well, in his 1905 semi-annual report to the Board of Health, Duncan listed among the eighteen toxicological analyses he had performed:

Stomach Contents, etc.—Coroner Strychnine present
Bicarbonate of Soda—Coroner Strychnine present
Medicine—Coroner Nux vomica present[7]

When Jordan wrote to President Wilbur in 1921 to give him his personal account of Mrs. Stanford's death, he mentioned that the government analyst had found "a small amount of strychnine" in the bicarbonate of soda and traces in Mrs. Stanford's stomach. Jordan explained that he had not actually seen the strychnine analyses, that "they were thus reported to me."[8] Yet it is certain that he had seen the analyses, because he had calculated the concentration of strychnine in the soda from Shorey's data—"one part in 1324," an amount too small, in his opinion, for a serious murderer to have used.[9] Jordan then went on to inform Wilbur that the chemist had been discharged from government employment.

President Jordan manipulated the words in Jared Smith's letters to draw the conclusion: "dismissed from the Government service for fraudulent analyses." Although the charge reinforced his case that the strychnine diagnosis was the product of a complex conspiracy, Jordan's portrayal of Shorey's career was, simply stated, untrue. It is quite possible that Smith's claims about Shorey's integrity were also false. If he thought Shorey such an untrustworthy scoundrel, why had Smith used Shorey's tables of chemical analyses in his own publications?[10]

If his reports were fraudulent, how could Shorey's discoveries of organic nitrogen compounds in Hawaiian soils have been confirmed years later by the station scientists W. P. Kelley and William McGeorge?[11] More important, why did Smith write in his 1907 report: "The former chemist, Mr. E. C. Shorey, was transferred to the Bureau of Soils, US Department of Agriculture?"[12] As it turned out, this was Jared Smith's last report; a few months after Shorey's departure, Smith also left the station, to enter the private sector as a tobacco grower. And Van Dine left shortly thereafter.

As a matter of fact, rather than being the dishonest and disgraced chemist portrayed by President Jordan, Dr. Shorey enjoyed a distinguished career in government service for the next thirty years. He worked in Washington, D.C., at the Bureau of Soils, becoming chief of the Division of Chemical Investigation. After an interlude at the Allied Dye and Chemical Company during and immediately after World War I, he was appointed senior biochemist in the Research Division of the

Department of Agriculture, a post he held until his retirement in 1935 at the age of sixty-nine. He died four years later, active to the end in his professional societies. Queen's University showed pride in her graduate when the *Queen's Alumni Review* recounted Shorey's career and his epoch-making scientific work, his eminence "in the counsels of the United States government."[13]

Despite a heavy work load, he always had time for his junior associates—"Ask Shorey" was the advice when a perplexing scientific question arose. Reading his publications on soils chemistry reveals Dr. Shorey's scientific integrity and strict adherence to his doctrine that only by its crystals can a precipitate be identified with certainty. One understands his position in Mrs. Stanford's case: a color reaction is insufficient.

Dr. Jordan's Charges

In addition to disparaging Dr. Shorey, Jordan also attacked Dr. Humphris in his 1921 letter to President Wilbur, in which he not only told how he planned to treat Jane Stanford's death in his autobiography, but also put on the record his version of her death—the "simple explanations which the facts permit":

In the night she awoke with agonizing pain, believing that she had been poisoned. . . . Her secretary, Miss Bertha Berner and her lady's maid, a Miss Hunt, gave her emetics, in spite of which, in great pain, but without rigor, she died during the night. The attendant physician, Dr. Humphries [*sic*] if I recall the name (an English remittance man, if not of good reputation) seemed dazed, as if under the influence of some drug. He tasted the bottle of soda and said something to the effect that it contained strychnine enough to kill a dozen men.[14]

The account borders on fiction. Agonizing pain and death without rigor were clinical points important to the diagnosis Jordan clung to—ruptured coronary artery—but they were not features of Mrs. Stanford's death. Humphris's actions on the night of her death, fully confirmed by Berner and Hunt, had been decisive, swift, and directed, not those of a dazed and drugged physician. Humphris did not have a bad reputation; rather, he enjoyed a successful referral practice. In fact, Jordan was verifiably correct on one point only: Dr. Humphris was English, from Yorkshire, where his father was a justice of the peace.

Dr. Humphris in Honolulu

Jordan was more discreet in his published writings, intimating only in *Days of a Man* that Humphris's lack of experience caused him to misdiagnose Mrs. Stanford's state of hysterical panic and become caught up in the charade of strychnine poisoning. In her memoir, Berner describes Humphris as "the hotel doctor," a tag that does not connote high professional attainment. No chronicler of Mrs. Stanford's death has challenged these characterizations.

Some of Humphris's professional credentials would have been known to Jordan from the coroner's inquest report: he was a fellow of the Royal College of Physicians of Edinburgh; a member of the Royal College of Surgeons of England; and a licentiate of the Royal College of Physicians of London. His reputation in Honolulu could have easily been discovered by inquiry. Humphris's broad interests in medicine—especially in neurology, dermatology, gynecology, and rheumatic and infectious diseases—his meticulous and compassionate care, and a lifelong scientific curiosity characterized his practice.

These traits he owed "to my father whose affectionate encouragement has always stimulated me to fresh endeavors," Humphris wrote years later in dedicating one of his books.[15] Support from his father had consisted of love and faith, not remittances. Humphris's scientific and humanistic approaches to medical practice would not fail to be applauded today: he sought "to bring qualities of common sense, watchfulness and deduction to bear upon each case offered for treatment, and to treat the patient and not the disease." And when he wrote, "Reading a text-book (or for that matter, a library of text-books) will not do everything. There is always the personal equation," could he have been thinking of Dr. Waterhouse and Mrs. Stanford?[16]

Humphris was to gain an enduring niche in the then growing field of electrotherapy, for him in 1905 an intense interest and an important component of his practice. He was caught up in galvanism and faradism, static brush and static wave discharges, the science of Nikola Tesla, and the pioneering clinical applications of Professor William Morton and Dr. William Snow. Humphris had come to Honolulu with his bride, Ethel, in 1898 and had joined Dr. George Herbert, first at the Oahu Insane Asylum and later in private practice. By 1902, he was thinking and writing about electrotherapy.

Humphris was a student of electrical, and later of X-ray, thermal, and ultraviolet energies in medical therapy, not a quack like some who shocked their patients indiscriminately with faradic electric batteries ordered from Waite and Bartlett's catalogue. Whereas most medical leaders agitated for legislation against quacks, Humphris was certain they would be vanquished by science. In his presidential address at the twenty-third annual meeting of the American Electro-Therapeutic Association in 1913, he advised his colleagues that "we as a scientific body must let quacks alone, and rather, by our example and our precept, secure to ourselves such a meed of recognition from our colleagues and the public that electro-therapeutic quackery, like Lewis Carroll's snark, will 'softly and silently vanish away.'"[17] Strangely enough, Dr. Jordan might have taken the same approach.

Humphris was also not a man devoid of personal reputation, as in Dr. Jordan's calumny. He was actually a very popular member of the Honolulu medical community of thirty-four physicians, most of whom were members of the Hawaiian Territorial Medical Society. He was always cheerful and buoyant, "born to smile at life," remembered a long-time friend when Frank Humphris passed away.[18] Even his moustache, waxed and twisted up in the style of Kaiser Wilhelm II, seemed to smile. He attended medical society meetings, regularly arranged banquet dinners and after-dinner entertainment at annual meetings, chaired committees, and presented papers on a broad range of topics.

Perhaps the most provocative paper read at the annual meeting of the Territorial Medical Society in November, 1906 was Humphris's "What Is Pain? An Attempt to Define Its Origin and Nature."[19] Working from examples of chronic painful maladies in his practice, Humphris developed a unifying hypothesis that pain was the result of pressure. Pressure on nerve endings or trunks, whether from trauma, tumor, infection or cellular edema, caused an altered electrical resistance in the nerve, the subjective manifestation of which was pain. Reaction to the paper was guarded: one doctor thought the case unproven; another thought the topic metaphysical; a third asked why the sharp end of a needle should cause more pain than the dull end.

Dr. Waterhouse, back from Malaya, argued that the topic was rooted in psychology, not metaphysics. He thought Humphris's paper "answered very well the question 'What is the *cause* of pain?' but did not answer the question which was the title of the paper, namely 'What *is* Pain?'[emphasis added]." Pain is a matter for the brain alone, Waterhouse insisted: "an hysterical person may have pain which is purely mental." Humphris apologized that the thrust of his paper was unclear to Dr. Waterhouse; he was more concerned with the peripheral physical phenomena, with high-frequency oscillations and Pascal's law.[20]

Waterhouse's reaction to the paper showed his interest in psychology, and, in particular, hysteria. His later discussion of Dr. I. Katsuki's paper "Suggestion and Suggestibility" was nearly as lengthy as Katsuki's presentation. Waterhouse reminisced over the case of a small child with cyclical abdominal swelling from a "phantom tumor" whom he had seen on pediatric rounds with the famous Dr. Abraham Jacobi when a student at Columbia. That both the girl's parents had died of abdominal tumors was the unusual etiological explanation Waterhouse gave for the child's malady.

Then he described at length a patient from his own practice, a young woman with attacks of hysterical coma, who had once taken a fall and unconsciously simulated the deformity of Colles's wrist fracture, in sympathetic harmony with a friend who had just been brought to Queen's Hospital with the same type of fracture. Waterhouse's hysterical patient was "more or less loose jointed." Once more, we must wonder if Waterhouse's conception of Mrs. Stanford's hysteria included a histrionic spasm.

He closed his overly long discussion of the Katsuki paper with a gibe at Humphris: "Mental suggestion is no doubt very efficacious ... in allaying pain with an organic basis for pain is certainly mental and of the mind (with apologies to Dr. Humphris who says that 'pain is pressure')."[21]

Dr. Humphris in London

That same year, 1908, Humphris was elected vice-president of the Hawaiian Territorial Medical Society, to succeed to the presidency in 1909.[22] Now forty-two years old, he began to realize that Honolulu could not provide the resources he required to mature in his specialty. Each year he had had to travel to the East Coast of the United States to attend the premier convention of electrotherapists, where the latest knowledge was exchanged and professional colleagues were engaged. Shortly after assuming the presidency, Dr. Humphris therefore decided to return to London to pursue advanced training, resigned from office, and embarked on the SS *Mongolia,* bound for San Francisco.

"Nothing but my absence from the Territory for a very extended period (at least) would cause me to resign," he wrote his colleagues from aboard ship. "My relations with the Society have ever been of so cordial a nature and my sense of gratification at the honor of the position I am now resigning so extreme that nothing but simple minded sorrow accompanies this resignation."[23] Dr. Humphris was among those "sincere, conscientious, and dedicated medical professionals who were well-educated and up-to-date," Dr. Ann Catts has observed, citing his letter of resignation as an example of the high social standards then prevailing.[24]

An assistantship in radiology and electrotherapeutics at the West London Hospital served Frank Humphris well. He spent the rest of his life observing, treating, writing, and teaching. He was the first foreign physician to be elected president of the American Electro-Therapeutic Association. The successor society, the American Congress of Rehabilitation Medicine, honored him with one of its first Gold Key Awards in 1932.

Humphris's work extended well beyond electrotherapy—to texts on actinotherapy and physiotherapy running through multiple editions, and to a stream of papers on a wide range of topics, a prolificity interrupted only by World War I, when he saw distinguished service as a major in the Egyptian Expeditionary Force. Even during the war, he learned and taught: a radiographic technique to locate shrapnel,[25] a paraffin bath for treatment of wounded limbs,[26] for example.

His text on actinotherapy, *Artificial Sunlight and Its Therapeutic Uses,* was the first English work on the subject, one that he summarized for the members of the venerable Hunterian Society when he was its president in 1925, in the society's 106th year. For several years, Humphris had urged the use of phototherapy in preventive medicine "not only to keep [people] fit, but to make them fitter than they are, to maintain or create that feeling of well being which should be ever present in each human body, to enable it to feel the joy of work, the joy indeed of just being alive."[27]

Humphris had particularly strong views on prophylactic phototherapy of pregnant women in order to prevent the vitamin D deficiency disease, congenital rickets. He campaigned passionately that its prevention was "a national duty . . . [to bring up a population] who will be sturdier and stronger by elimination of a disease which, for too long, has weakened and depleted the peoples of many races." Dr. Jordan would surely have benefited from association with Dr. Humphris.[28]

F. Howard Humphris died at Bath, England, on June 17, 1947, aged eighty-one.[29] His textbooks are preserved in the special collection of works on electrotherapy of the Bakken Library and Museum in Minneapolis, founded by a later electrotherapist, Earl Bakken, inventor of the cardiac pacemaker. Humphris has also not been forgotten in Hawaii; his paper "Electricity in the Relief of Pain," read at the November 1908 meeting of the Territorial Medical Society, was recently reprinted in the health periodical *Healing Island*.[30]

9 ⌒ The Other Physicians

Dr. Harry Murray

A brief sketch of the other physicians directly involved in Mrs. Stanford's case should suffice to show that President Jordan's notion of a conspiracy was preposterous. As rational men and women would have realized at the time, the plot would at the very least have had to involve, not only Drs. Humphris, Murray, Day, and Wood, but also Drs. Pratt, Sawyer, and Taylor, the chemists Shorey and Duncan, Judge Stanley, the Stanford representative, Deputy Sheriff Rawlins, High Sheriff Henry, and the undertaker, Henry Williams. Then a stratagem would have had to germinate in the early morning hours of March 1 and propagate to engage all the co-conspirators by day's end. Such an idea cannot be seriously entertained by even the most ardent conspiracy theorist.

Jordan had warned Judge Carl Smith to keep an eye on Humphris and Murray, to look into their past practices. Whether Judge Smith did so has not been recorded. Not long after he completed his other services to the president, Smith returned to his law practice at Hilo.

Harry Murray (the newspapers usually called him Harvey, for some reason) was a popular man who lacked a notorious past. He hailed from Pictou, Nova Scotia, and clung proudly to his British citizenship throughout his life. He had come to Oahu in 1894 after medical school at the University of New York, internship at the Chambers Street Hospital in lower Manhattan, and postdoctoral training abroad in Edinburgh and London, where he might have crossed paths with Frank Humphris. In his first year of practice, Murray faced a major cholera epidemic in Honolulu (he is credited with diagnosing the first case), one to which native Hawaiians were especially susceptible. John Waterhouse, Ernest's father, was president of the Board of Health at the time and directed the efforts to contain the epidemic.

After seven years of successful medical practice, Murray sought a mainland opportunity and traveled to Shanghai to be the medical director of the Oriental Life Insurance Company. Honolulu drew him back in 1904, and except for military service, he remained in practice there until his death, honored by election to the presidency of the Hawaiian Territorial Medical Society in 1913. In 1917, aged fifty, Murray volunteered for service in the Canadian Army Medical Corps. He drew assignments of front-line medical duty in France and postwar medical responsibility in Belgium for English soldiers liberated from German prisons. Harry Murray died in 1920, less than a year after returning to Honolulu. At his funeral procession before the Catholic Cathedral, U.S. military detachments and British war veterans marched alongside the horse-drawn hearse, Murray's mount walking behind, saddled and with his boots reversed in the stirrups. Ironically, Dr. Murray had just been appointed to the Necrology Committee of the medical society.

Murray did scheme with his colleagues F. H. Humphris and L. E. Cofer on an unconventional arrangement for a banquet dinner at the seventeenth annual meeting of the Hawaiian Territorial Medical Society in November 1908. The three friends startled the membership with dining tables arrayed in the shape of a human body, the vertebrae represented by white carnations, the intestines by a convolution of red carnations, the legs straddling a human skeleton draped with red light bulbs. The menu became a collector's item: stomachics, meloncolics, aqua tortosa viridia for starters; pois(s)on, prepared ptomaines, Pasteur tuberoses and cholera morbus in wafers for entrees. The dinner may have been Humphris's idea; a friend remembered, "As a host he was second to none—his great delight in life was 'throwing a party.'"[1]

Dr. Francis Day and Dr. John Pratt

Dr. Francis Day died in 1906 at the age of forty-six. He had practiced in Honolulu for nearly twenty years, holding important offices in his profession—port physician in charge of enforcing vital quarantine policies, president of the Board of Health—and enriching his life as a violinist in the elite Cecelian Instrument Club. He was especially concerned with the plight of patients suffering from tuberculosis. After his death, the community established the Dr. Francis R. Day Memorial

Fund to provide a salary for a nurse who made home visits to patients with the illness. Day's role in the alleged plot was to emphasize the uniqueness of Mrs. Stanford's spasm, take notes of Wood's autopsy findings, and pack her heart and brain in specimen jars. In addition, of course, he confronted Ernest Waterhouse.

The *Pacific Commercial Advertiser* took notice of his death: "Possessed of a winning personality, Dr. Day was liked by even casual acquaintances. . . . Taking him all in all, there are few men among his contemporaries whose removal would create a more universally felt vacancy in the community."[2] It was hardly the description of someone bent on defrauding the Stanford estate. "Our doctor was dear old Francis R. Day," Dr. John Pratt's son wrote, reflecting on his own childhood sixty years later.[3]

Dr. John Pratt received the forensic evidence from Deputy Sheriff Rawlins in the early morning hours after Mrs. Stanford's death, debunking newspaper reports that Dr. and Mrs. Humphris sampled the bicarbonate of soda the following day, as well as Jordan's claim that the bottle of soda remained in Humphris's possession for "some hours."[4] Pratt had a long and honorable career in public health, serving for many years as the chief sanitary officer of the Territorial Board of Health. He was not mentioned as a conspirator.

Dr. Clifford Wood

Dr. Clifford Wood's role in the strychnine diagnosis was pivotal, of course, not so much because of what he found as because of what he did not. Stanford officials had objected to his having conducted the postmortem examination, complaining that the autopsy was the responsibility of a government physician appointed by the Board of Health. Government physicians, appointed to provide medical care to the indigent, once had the responsibility of performing autopsies in cases of death unattended by a physician, but the practice had ceased in 1903 when the legislature eliminated funding for the program. Humphris found the idea ludicrous: "Supposing . . . I had waited for the Territorial officials to undertake the autopsy, can you imagine what the Stanford estate people would have said?"[5]

Humphris was fully aware of Wood's experience as an autopsy surgeon. Before establishing a private practice with Francis Day, Wood had actually held several government positions in Hawaii—physician for the Koolaupoko district, Honolulu city physician, and member of the Board of Health. During the cholera epidemic of 1894 and the bubonic plague epidemic of 1899–1900, Dr. Wood had performed dozens of autopsies. Autopsies seemed endless in January 1900, when the plague ravaged Honolulu's Chinatown.

Wood, appointed president of the Board of Health that month, instituted tough measures to control the epidemic, which had started three weeks earlier and eventually caused sixty-one deaths. Burning infected houses (the classic medieval prophylaxis) in Chinatown helped bring the plague under control, but not before the entire Chinese community was accidentally destroyed on January 20, 1900. A shifting wind caused a conflagration that leveled nearly forty acres of homes and businesses. Wood took both criticism and praise for his public health tactics. "Though Dr. Wood has a stiff temper and an obstinate will, he possesses also a power of sympathy most invaluable to him as a physician and a man," the *Pacific Commercial Advertiser* noted.[6]

Clifford Wood had come to Hawaii in 1886 at the urging of his boyhood friend Francis Day. At the time of Mrs. Stanford's death, Wood was senior attending surgeon at Queen's Hospital. He had served as president of the Hawaiian Territorial Medical Society in 1898 and was again elected to that office in 1925. The governor appointed him president of the Board of Medical Examiners, and he became the first physician on the Board of Directors of Queen's Hospital. Wood was one of fifteen Hawaiian physicians featured in a contemporary historian's article, "Medical Men Who Helped Shape Hawaii."[7] Throughout his medical career, he concerned himself with issues of public health. His reminiscences at medical society meetings gave a clue to the beginning of his interest—nineteen medical school classmates had neglected to be vaccinated and had contracted smallpox. Wood died in 1939, at the age of seventy-nine.

Dr. Ernest Waterhouse

Of all the physicians involved in Mrs. Stanford's case, only Ernest Waterhouse—on whose judgment Dr. Jordan relied for proof of heart disease—failed to gain a reputation in the medical profession. "You need . . . a four years' course in medicine, two years in a hospital . . . with perhaps a year or so in Germany, and at least five years more to grow a beard and gain the confidence of the laity," he wrote in the Princeton triennial record.[8] Having completed that schedule in 1905, however (except for the beard), he turned his attention to rubber planting in Malaya. It was in this field that he made his reputation. When Waterhouse wrote of shaving "a thin slice . . . off the under margin of this incision, which re-opens the lactiferous ducts and starts the milk flowing again" in a lengthy article in the *Pacific Commercial Advertiser* published in August 1905, two days after his sensational exposure as Jordan's consultant, he was not describing a surgical procedure to relieve mammary gland inspissation but rather how one tapped a rubber tree; he had swapped his scalpel for a farrier's knife, the best instrument for incising rubber tree bark.[9]

Ernest Coniston Waterhouse was born a true cockney in 1871. That was the year his father, John, managed the London branch office of the John T. Waterhouse Company, the family mercantile firm based in Honolulu. His mother, Elizabeth, had come along to seek relief from homesickness. Elizabeth was the daughter of Thomas Pinder of the Pinder and Bourne china works in Burslem, Staffordshire. After she and John had married in England, they had honeymooned at Lake Coniston, from which Ernest derived his middle name.[10]

Ernest spent his childhood comfortably in Honolulu. His interest in a medical career did not seem to spring from his own family but rather from neighbors, the Judds. James Judd and Ernest were close in age, and James, inspired by his celebrated grandfather, Dr. Gerrit Judd, had always wanted to be a surgeon. Ernest went off to Princeton, James to Yale, and they ended up three classes apart at the Columbia College of Physicians and Surgeons. By 1903, the childhood friends were in medical practice together in Honolulu. While he was an intern at the General Memorial Hospital, Ernest had married a staff nurse, Helen Amy (Nellie) Harding, from Welsford, New Brunswick. The couple had three children.

Ernest is credited with being the first American to plant rubber in Malaya.[11] By the close of 1905, he had become president of the Pahang and the Tandjong Olak rubber companies. Both companies attracted investors when they were listed on the Honolulu Stock and Bond Exchange in 1909, and their profits skyrocketed.[12] Over the next two decades, Waterhouse held executive positions in four other rubber plantations. He spent much more time in Malaya and Sumatra than in his medical office, and his attendance at the monthly meetings of the Hawaiian Territorial Medical Association fell off sharply. His last meeting was in January 1909, when he nominated his partner, James Judd, to succeed Frank Humphris as president of the society. Waterhouse closed his medical practice for good in 1913.

Young Dr. Waterhouse had started his surgical career with promise. One of his early (although perhaps unrealized) ambitions, family legend has it, was to remove his own appendix. He is said to have performed the first aseptic surgical procedure in Hawaii in 1900, an abdominal hysterectomy. His techniques may well have introduced important changes in Queen's Hospital surgical policy, but there was a down side for Waterhouse. Being scrubbed for surgery necessitated his commanding nurses to open doors for him, and some colleagues considered the manner behind his orders arrogant. Might they have thought the same about his conclusion that Mrs. Stanford's terminal agony had been hysterical?

Gertrude Harding, Nellie Waterhouse's little sister, also found her brother-in-law arrogant when she joined his household in Honolulu in 1910. Accustomed to responsibilities on the family farm in New Brunswick, Gert soon tired of the social whirl of governor's receptions, dances, and moonlight swims at the Moana Hotel beach and took a job selling candy in a Portuguese coffeehouse. Livid over the implication that he was not a good provider, Waterhouse threatened to ship her back to Canada. When Gert's pony accidentally hanged herself, Waterhouse, rather than console the distraught young woman, ranted "get in touch with the Board of Health and find out what . . . [to] do with the body."[13]

It is unlikely that Waterhouse was aware of his sister-in-law's visits with an Episcopal priest to a slum dwelling, where she helped apply electrical currents to the muscles of a child paralyzed by poliomyelitis.[14] He would almost certainly have disapproved. Humphris, in contrast, would surely have applauded the electrotherapeutic effort to ameliorate the child's condition. It was a therapy in which he firmly believed (although he might have been critical of the primitive electrotherapeutic apparatus she used).[15] For Gert, the experience marked the beginning of a life devoted to social service.

Waterhouse's prosperity started to decline in 1920 with the severe postwar slump in rubber prices. On a trip to Honolulu in 1923, although outwardly optimistic that the British cap on exports of Malayan rubber would stabilize prices in the long term, he painted a gloomy picture of his Hawaiian Sumatra Plantation, which specialized in rubber, hardwood lumber, and coffee. On February 16, he reported in the *Pacific Commercial Advertiser*: "the rubber trees are just beginning to produce . . . the [hardwood] trees are so far apart that lumbering is an expensive proposition . . . [and the] coffee has been badly hit by various rusts and blight."[16] The very next day, Waterhouse lost control of his car on the Diamond Head road while driving home from a dinner party at Kahala. Nellie was thrown from the car and died instantly of a broken neck; Ernest suffered cuts and bruises.[17]

Waterhouse's fortunes changed for the worse not long thereafter: two costly marriages ended in divorce; he squandered his money in poor investments; and the jobs he took failed to be sustaining. For the last ten years of his life, he lived in a transients' hotel on O'Farrell Street in San Francisco's Tenderloin district. His brother found him there in 1947, selling newspapers on the street, destitute and sick. He was hospitalized at the Stanford Lane Hospital (Stanford Medical School's principal teaching hospital), where he died nine days later, in his seventy-fifth year. The death certificate listed as his usual occupations: "Physician, Rubber Co., Clothing Salesman." He left an estate consisting of stock certificates worth about $125.

It is doubtful whether Dr. Waterhouse ever knew that history had largely accepted his diagnosis of the cause of Mrs. Stanford's death.

PART THREE

10 ⌒ Perpetuating the Myth

In his biography of David Starr Jordan, Edward Burns writes, "Though he made mistakes and was occasionally the target of bitter complaints from his subordinates, he came to be regarded over the years as a figure of heroic proportions."[1] Thus, it is not surprising that few have challenged Jordan's version of how Jane Stanford died. In the foreword to his autobiography, Jordan informs readers that he "rarely mentions any one of whom he must speak disparagingly."[2] In recounting the story of Mrs. Stanford's death, he says only that her false belief that she had been poisoned misled an inexperienced attending physician, that the correct diagnosis of coronary artery rupture was made by the well-informed physician Dr. E. C. Waterhouse and confirmed by surgeons at Cooper Medical College.

Jordan mentions neither the strychnine-laced bicarbonate of soda nor the episode of poisoning in San Francisco. Possibly the brevity of his account followed a recommendation by Bertha Berner that he avoid controversy. (She is said to have advised him to omit reference to the notorious dismissal of Professor Edward Ross from his autobiography, which he did.) It would be on Berner's memoir that historians would come to rely. In fact, Orrin Elliott, in *Stanford University: The First Twenty-five Years*, although he refers to the Poland water episode, merely mentions the date and place of Mrs. Stanford's death and defers to Bertha Berner for details.[3]

Berner's memoir has provided the foundation for most subsequent accounts of Mrs. Stanford's poisonings. Remarkably, although Berner gives much detail, however erroneous, about the Poland water poisoning, there is a dearth of information bearing on the final episode in Honolulu. What little she writes is largely fictitious. In addition to describing fanciful actions of the physicians ("The hotel doctor now hurried in with a stomach pump, but the other doctor put up his hand and held him back"),[4] she leaves out virtually everything of importance that transpired afterward—the inquest, the report of the coroner's jury, and the fact that she had laid out the dose of bicarbonate of soda containing the strychnine that Mrs. Stanford ingested. For Berner, only the Jordan investigation and the Ophüls report factor into the cause of Mrs. Stanford's death. And Berner's ambiguous writings are the only sources for the Ophüls report.

In *Stanford: The Story of a University*, Edith Mirrielees, who had been a Stanford undergraduate when Mrs. Stanford was poisoned, deviated little from the Berner history, although she acknowledged that the Honolulu police had every reason to suspect murder because of the earlier Poland water poisoning. Expanding on a phrase from Berner's memoir, Mirrielees writes, "it was finally determined that the bottle, emptied of its original contents, had been refilled with cleaning fluid and left in the room by mistake."[5] The Poland water poisoning thus explained, Mirrielees's case appears stronger when she concludes, "Dr. Jordan had asserted before he left for Honolulu that the symptoms were not those of strychnine poisoning and after a fortnight of hysteria, all but the morbid-minded came to agree. In the faculty and among the older alumni, quiet took the place of shuddering speculation."

One older alumnus, Judge George Crothers, continued to believe that Mrs. Stanford had been poisoned. Because of the closeness of his relationship with Mrs. Stanford, he was fully aware of the Poland water episode of January 14, 1905. She had told him, he recalled many years later, that President Jordan had suggested the bitterness in the water might have been from strychnine and that an analysis was warranted.[6] On the day she sailed for Honolulu, Mrs. Stanford wrote to Crothers about the "peculiar circumstances" of her departure, "horrified that any human beings feel that they have been injured to such an extent as to desire to revenge themselves in a way so heroic as has happened."[7] The letter was among her last.

When Crothers wrote to Cora Older in 1947 to respond to the author's request for information about Mrs. Stanford's death, he did not doubt that "someone must have been guilty of attempting to poison Mrs. Stanford about the middle of January, 1905." As well, he felt certain that Mrs. Stanford had taken bicarbonate of soda containing strychnine in Honolulu, but that "she would have obtained only one-

eleventh of a grain, and . . . this would not have been a lethal dose."
Nevertheless, he wrote of the event as "the second poisoning incident."
He recalled that Berner had later told him that a physician in India had
supplied the bicarbonate of soda. "Any American physician," he
thought, "would have insisted on the ingredients being properly measured, mixed and supplied in separate paper containers." To avoid the
suggestion that Miss Berner might have been guilty of wrongdoing, he
advised Mrs. Older not to go into the matter of Mrs. Stanford's death.[8]

Mrs. Older did not resist including the sensational story in her book,
San Francisco: Magic City, published after the death of Judge Crothers.
She drew heavily on the information he had supplied but further obfus-
cated history with an embellishment that the Indian physician who had
supposedly supplied the bicarbonate of soda to Mrs. Stanford had
added strychnine because he thought it was good for her indigestion.
"Perhaps it was a carelessly prepared prescription," Older theorizes.[9]
Or, perhaps, respecting Crothers's concern, she sought to deflect suspicion from Miss Berner. Mrs. Older repeated a small detail that Crothers had mentioned in his letter: the Poland water contained crystals of
strychnine; the bicarbonate of soda contained powdered strychnine.
That two different preparations of strychnine were involved in Mrs.
Stanford's poisonings does not appear to have attracted attention or
raised implications. The poisoner(s) clearly possessed both rodent and
medicinal grade strychnine.

Given George Crothers's conviction that Mrs. Stanford had been
poisoned twice, it is surprising that his law associate and biographer,
Henry C. Clausen, also adheres to Berner's memoir when he reports,
"there was no evidence whatever of poisoning [in Honolulu] . . . a
cleaning solution had been put into an empty bottle for cleaning purposes but was taken to Mrs. Stanford by mistake [in San Francisco]."[10]
It is not known if he wondered why rodent poison would be in a
cleaning solution. Mr. Clausen seems to have been so intent on avoid-
ing the poisoning controversy that in reproducing Mrs. Stanford's last
letter to Judge Crothers, he omitted the paragraph about her going
away under peculiar circumstances.

Clausen, like the chroniclers who preceded him, did not have access
to the Jane Lathrop Stanford case files of the Hawaii attorney general
and could have learned only from reading contemporaneous newspaper
accounts that Mrs. Stanford's autopsy had revealed the presence of

strychnine in her body. In late 1967, the Stanford University Libraries obtained a copy of the case files, giving Dr. Gunther Nagel ready access to the inquest testimony, the autopsy report, and the chemical analyses. In his fine tribute to Mrs. Stanford, first published in 1975 as *Jane Stanford: Her Life and Letters*, in which he reveals her remarkable strength of character and resolve, Nagel drew from the official documents to construct a more detailed account of what transpired in room 120 of the Moana Hotel.

Slight embellishments—"An emetic was given with good effect, followed by a hypodermic injection"—did not detract from his more informative account. Nagel revealed that traces of strychnine were found in Mrs. Stanford's bicarbonate of soda and in her "stomach" contents. But he then dismissed those findings in favor of what he called Dr. Jordan's and Mr. Hopkins's exhaustive pursuit of the truth, during which "they learned that the government analyst . . . *was shortly afterward dismissed for fraudulent analysis* [emphasis added]."[11]

Nagel gave no credence to the conclusions of the Honolulu physicians; strengthened Miss Berner's rendering of the Ophüls report by using parentheses instead of brackets around the emendatory clause; and, quoting Dr. Jordan's letter to President Wilbur, published Jordan's libelous characterization of Dr. Humphris for the first time. A subsequent reviewer of Nagel's book removed any lingering ambiguity about the diagnosis: the chemist had been dismissed for fraudulent analysis "in another case"; the Ophüls group had found "chronic heart disease resulting from partial obstruction of blood vessels."[12]

That same year, 1975, Luther Spoehr, a graduate student in Stanford's Department of History, submitted his dissertation on aspects of Dr. Jordan's presidency. The history student, decidedly not a fan of the president, drew heavily on archival sources to document the facts surrounding the summary dismissal of Professor Goebel and the subsequent severe criticism of Jordan by leading academicians. Surprisingly, he did not review primary documents when writing about Mrs. Stanford's death. Despite having called attention to rumors of foul play, Spoehr concluded: "the official verdict was that she died of a ruptured coronary artery," citing Jordan's autobiography and Berner's memoir.[13]

Several recent chroniclers of Mrs. Stanford's death have concluded that her two closely spaced encounters with strychnine logically beg a diagnosis of murder.[14] Household jealousies, cleaning solution substitutions, prescription errors notwithstanding, to them it stretches credibility that Mrs. Stanford could have been administered strychnine twice in six weeks without a murderous intent. Each of these authors has re-marked on Dr. Jordan's efforts to promote an alternative cause of death, and each has concluded that he did so out of concern for the reputation of the university, out of a sense of duty to avoid scandal.

11 ⪻ Summing Up

Case Closed

From clinical grounds alone there can be little doubt that Mrs. Stanford died in the suffocating grip of a tetanic spasm characteristic of strychnine poisoning. Coupled with the Poland water poisoning six weeks earlier, and the forensic evidence that the bicarbonate of soda she ingested contained strychnine, the diagnosis grows in certainty. When it is understood that strychnine is not an ingredient of bicarbonate of soda, the conclusion that Mrs. Stanford was murdered is difficult to avoid.[1]

Dr. Waterhouse may have flirted tentatively with that realization, a botched murder attempt perhaps, when he wrote to President Jordan just before departing for Ceylon:

It makes no difference whether we accept the hypothesis that someone put the crystals of strychnine in the Poland water, and thinking (however erroneously) that Mrs. Stanford was not poisoned on account of the fact that she vomited the Poland water (because there was so *much* strychnine in it) and therefore, when making a second attempt, decided to make the dose *small* and not being up on dosage put in only a medicinal dose after all . . . still [she] did not die from strychnine poisoning [underlining in original].[2]

Regardless of Dr. Waterhouse's persistent opinion and Dr. Jordan's concurrence that the dose of strychnine was medicinal, for Mrs. Stanford it was fatal.

It seems remarkable today that the considered opinions of the attending and autopsy physicians, the toxicologists, the Honolulu police department, and the coroner's jury could be so easily dismissed on the basis of a brief declaration by President Jordan and Trustee Hopkins that Mrs. Stanford died of natural causes. Failing even to acknowledge the Poland water poisoning, their claim was not supported by any new clue, medical or forensic evidence, or expert testimony that the poisoning diagnosis was "without foundation." Though their statement in the press asserted that a diagnosis of poisoning was incompatible with evidence in their possession, such evidence, as far as is known, consisted of the poorly informed opinions of Dr. Waterhouse and Mr. Callundan. No other evidence was ever presented to the public, or, in all likelihood, to law enforcement officials.

During the two-week period between Mrs. Stanford's death and Jordan's press release, the police developed a suspect list, conducted intensive interrogations, and searched the San Francisco mansion and the servants' effects. Bertha Berner, although at first a leading suspect, was rapidly exonerated on the basis of attestations of her long and deep devotion to Mrs. Stanford. Berner was questioned in her hotel room in Honolulu, always in the presence of a legal representative of Stanford, but she did not undergo the repeated intense grilling at police headquarters as had Richmond, Ah Wing, and Beverly. For the San Francisco police to have closed the Stanford case never having interrogated Miss Berner also seems remarkable in that she was the only person present at both poisoning events.

Spillane, Burnett, Morse, and Callundan remarked frequently during their brief flurry of investigation that they were stymied by lack of motive. As Jordan explained to Shorey, "[Mrs. Stanford] had not an enemy in the world, and there is no one who could possibly have gained anything by her death."[3] The failure of Callundan to discover a motive was the key factor in the Morse Agency's closing the case.

Dr. Jordan's Cover-Up

President Jordan's efforts to prove that Mrs. Stanford died of some form of heart disease resulted in a cover-up that continued for nearly two decades. Over this period of time, he gave poorly conceived explanations, engaged in seemingly senseless fabrications, and formulated egregious charges for which there was no evidence.

For example, the cable he hastily composed for the Associated Press to the effect that Bertha Berner had found the bicarbonate of soda harmless and tasteless did not accord with his press release stating that the soda had contained a medicinal amount of strychnine. Even a medicinal quantity of the poison would have stimulated Berner's taste buds, which could be expected to detect a dilution of strychnine of one part in 100,000. As Jordan is said to have informed Mrs. Stanford, strychnine is "the bitterest thing in the world."[4]

The incongruity of these statements could be widely appreciated, but other claims were privately expressed and made no obvious sense. Why did he tell Waterhouse that he had revealed his identity to Humphris? Why did he write Wilbur that he had not seen Shorey's analytical results? Why did he tell Jared Smith that he had no reason to doubt Shorey's analysis and then shortly afterward suggest that Shorey had colluded with Humphris? Why did he refer to Richmond as a temporary maid? How could these peripheral untruths fortify his cover-up, unless they spread word-of-mouth? His claim that reexamination of Mrs. Stanford's organs revealed a rupture of the aorta was at least central to the cover-up, even though transparently false in light of the coroner's inquest.

Almost without exception, Jordan's libelous derogations appeared in private correspondence. That they were effective in shaping history has been shown. The occasional disparaging remark appearing in the press he simply denied and attributed to fanciful reporting.

To explain the strychnine in the bicarbonate of soda, Jordan germinated the idea that it had been placed there by Humphris. The charge, absurd on face value and decidedly malicious, is also countered by the facts. Humphris would have required an opportunity to do such a thing. It is not likely that, aroused from sleep, he dashed to Mrs. Stanford's room with a vial of strychnine in his pocket. Jordan portrayed the physician's tampering as a more fully considered action when he told Judge Leib that "the carbonate . . . was for some hours in the possession of Dr. Humphris."[5] Yet according to sworn testimony, Humphris had at once relinquished the bottles of soda and cascara to Day and Murray, and they, in turn, had given the medicines over to Deputy Sheriff Rawlins when he arrived at the Moana Hotel. The carbonate had not been in Humphris's possession for some hours.

It is difficult to understand what prompted Jordan to bring up the case long after investigations had terminated and Mrs. Stanford's natural death had been accepted: the press interview in December 1905; the request of the Board of Trustees in September 1906; and the elaborately false account conveyed to President Wilbur in 1921. Did these renewals respond to external events or to inner obsessions that called for reinforcing explanations? What construction explains the thoughts and actions of the president?

Did President Jordan distort the truth, perhaps in agreement with the wishes and instructions of Stanford executors, to preserve the dignity of both the life and death of the greatly beloved benefactress, as some have suggested? Would it have offended sensibilities, when remembering Mrs. Stanford, to know that her life had ended violently? Admittedly, it is difficult to project oneself into the crisis of the time, but on reflection it is disturbing to think that those who loved Mrs. Stanford would chart such a dishonorable course. To cover up her poisoning would mean trivializing the anxious depression she suffered for six weeks and shrugging off the agony of her death. A murderer would remain at large; Mrs. Stanford would be denied justice and respect for her courage; and the loved ones would never gain certain closure, to use the modern term.

Perhaps Jordan convinced himself that the results of Callundan's investigations and Waterhouse's consultation pointed *in the direction* of death by natural causes but were not *conclusive*? "If I believed that a murder had been committed," Jordan had written, "I should favor following the matter to the end regardless of the cost in money and strength."[6] Had he thus pursued this end with resolve but come up short, finding it impossible to prove that one of the suspects had put strychnine in Mrs. Stanford's water or bicarbonate of soda? Yet the strychnine was there, quantified and characterized chemically. Were Jordan truly convinced of her natural death, someone, he must have thought, added the poison after the fact. Why not Richmond for the water and Humphris for the soda? Could Dr. Jordan have sought to expose Richmond as crazy and Humphris as a disreputable extortionist in an attempt to solidify what he firmly believed to be the correct diagnosis, and to convince skeptics that his conclusion was correct? Casting aspersions on Shorey would be a natural extension of this strategy. As Luther Spoehr put it, Jordan had a "terrifying capacity for convincing himself that what he wanted was right."[7]

Could Dr. Jordan have lied in order to protect someone from suspicion—Bertha Berner, perhaps, who was promptly targeted by the newspapers as the leading suspect because she was the only one to have been present at both poisonings? In his request of the Board of Trustees for a disclosure of the facts proving natural death, Jordan argued for justice—to the truth, to the memory of Mrs. Stanford, and to "Miss Bertha Berner, who has suffered the tortures of trial by newspaper, and whose reputation can be cleared only by the publication of the actual facts."[8] But aside from the impulsive finger-pointing of reporters in the days immediately following Mrs. Stanford's death, there is no evidence that Berner continued to be tried by the newspapers. The press, like the coroner's jury, had long before exonerated Miss Berner.

Might President Jordan have considered it important to protect the university campus from intrigue, to forestall the gossiping of Eastern academicians? Stanford University was still recovering from the adverse consequences of the firing of Professor Ross (see Appendix 2). Whether the professor's dismissal was the misguided action of Mrs. Stanford, President Jordan, or both, many educators were concerned that academic freedom had been trampled on at Stanford, that *die Luft der Freiheit* no longer blew.[9]

If protecting the campus from scandal factored in President Jordan's plan to promote a natural cause for Mrs. Stanford's demise, the strategy was ineffectual. Jordan's summary dismissal of Professor Goebel would soon attract more negative attention than ever, compelling Harvard President Charles W. Eliot to write to Jordan: "I think I differ from you fundamentally on the nature of the responsibility of a university president. In my judgment he should be absolutely a constitutional and not a despotic ruler."[10] It is important to examine the cases of Professors Ross and Goebel when trying to fathom the reasons behind Jordan's cover-up.

Little more than two months after Mrs. Stanford's funeral, the San Francisco newspapers engaged in a flurry of reporting on President Jordan's firing of Professor Julius Goebel, Mrs. Stanford's friend and confidant. The temporal relationship between Mrs. Stanford's death and Professor Goebel's dismissal has been revealed by W. B. Carnochan (see Appendix 3).[11] News reporters had difficulty ascertaining the facts underlying the firing because Dr. Jordan had left for a summer vacation in Europe, and Goebel's whereabouts were unknown.

The professor's attorney, William Denman, provided important background information. Several years earlier, Goebel (and thirty-six other faculty and staff) had signed an open letter to the Friends of Stanford University asserting that Professor Ross's dismissal was justified and had not infringed on his right of academic freedom, but the letter was not critical of Ross. The trouble for Goebel began, Mr. Denman said, when he opposed a resolution "to besmirch Ross'[s] name in Dr.

Jordan's behalf."[12] The *San Francisco Chronicle* column header pin-pointed the animus between president and professor more explicitly: "Also States That Whole Case Is Result of a Criticism of University's Management He Wrote for Mrs. Stanford."[13]

In fact, on June 6, 1904, Goebel had written Mrs. Stanford, at her insistence, to give his frank assessment of the damaging effects of the Ross affair on faculty recruitment; the political patronage and favoritism that characterized the administrative style of President Jordan; and the anxiety of the younger faculty and potential recruits that if they did not toe the line of loyalty to the president, they risked losing their positions. He thought the conditions "a disgrace to scholarship and they must be remedied at once, if your plans of a great University are to be carried out at all."[14]

Mrs. Stanford had been deeply hurt by the Ross affair and she was troubled by Goebel's disclosures as she confided a few weeks later to her old friend and senior trustee Horace Davis:

we are "bound hand and foot" because of the great mistakes made in the Ross affair and are obliged to keep in our present condition. The President's range of selection is limited . . . to a certain section, and Stanford is virtually a branch of Cornell and Indiana University, and presents opportunities for friendly acts of accommodation not always conducive to the greatest benefit, to the important work we have so seriously in mind to do. This has been painfully evident to me for a long time.[15]

She sent Davis a confidential report she had prepared for the Board of Trustees (she had also shown parts of the report to Crothers) and asked for his advice.

Although we do not know the thrust of her report, Crothers told Registrar Orrin Elliott many years later that Mrs. Stanford had written several memoranda to the board requesting that it force Jordan's retirement. At the time she relinquished her administrative authority she had pledged a majority of the board to this goal.[16] Crothers had persuaded her not to force the issue, fearing quite correctly that serious chaos would result. But in sympathy with some of her views, less than a week before Mrs. Stanford's death, he had conveyed his own concerns to board president Samuel Leib, suggesting that Jordan be "cautioned against giving color to the claim that he is 'smoking out' all of the members of the Faculty who do not agree, without comment, in all his policies."[17]

According to Spoehr, "rumors abounded that Mrs. Stanford planned to replace Jordan . . . when she returned from a vacation . . . the gossips always considered it fortuitous for Jordan that in Honolulu, on February 28, 1905, Mrs. Stanford died."[18] Even if the rumors had little basis, the president must have been aware of Mrs. Stanford's waning confidence in his leadership and her thoughts of removing him from office. Is it possible, then, that he wondered whether Professor Goebel, the trustees Leib, Davis, Crothers, Lathrop, and perhaps others might *suspect* he played a role in Mrs. Stanford's death and therefore sought to deflect their suspicion? Could this concern have recurred from time to time—exacerbated by circumstances difficult to discern—to prompt fresh avowals that Mrs. Stanford had died of natural causes?

The question must also be asked whether Dr. Jordan did, in fact, have a hand in the poisoning of Mrs. Stanford. But given the relationship of mutual respect that he and Mrs. Stanford had shared for so many years, and knowing that their differences most often found solution in compromise, it is hard to imagine that he saw murder as the answer to their increasingly inimical relationship. No evidence linked Jordan to the poisonings; there is no basis for a belief that he constructed the cover-up to conceal his own guilt.

Some readers may believe that Dr. Jordan wrote and told the plain truth about Mrs. Stanford's death and the events leading to it: that the servants, driven by jealousy of Bertha Berner and determined to turn Mrs. Stanford against her, conspired to put poison in the Poland water in San Francisco; that Elizabeth Richmond, her mind deranged by a fit of mania, and her will fueled by successes in the houses of British aristocracy, was the poisoner; that the physicians and senior law officers of Honolulu, summoned hastily in the dark of night, at once recognized an opportunity for lucrative extortion by concocting a poisoning death; that each agreed to perjure himself before the coroner's jury with lies so consistent they would be difficult to detect; that Dr. Shorey helped by falsifying the chemical analyses; and that Dr. Humphris had degenerated into a disreputable and incompetent hotel doctor, lost the respect of the medical community, and taken refuge in drugs.

It is hoped that the new information provided here will help dispel such a belief for the sake of all the participants in the tragedy, not the least to do justice to the final agonizing struggle of the Mother of the University, Jane Lathrop Stanford. David Starr Jordan writes in *Days of A Man* about the "false rumor" that she had been poisoned: "This had its origin in the fact that she herself, waking in the night in great agony, believed such to be the case."[19] I concur with Mrs. Stanford.

Appendixes

☞ Dr. Shorey and
the Experiment Station

The Hawaii Agricultural Experiment Station was a research and educational facility established by the U.S. Congress with a mandate to examine crop-growing conditions and instruct local growers on sound agricultural practices. Jared Smith, an agriculturalist from the Section of Seed and Plant Introduction of the U.S. Department of Agriculture, directed the station as special agent in charge. Smith arrived in Hawaii in the spring of 1901 and recruited a workforce to clear the designated acreage in the Makiki Valley on the outskirts of Honolulu.[1] He constructed an architecturally attractive special agent's house of six rooms and wide verandas, shaded by an overhanging roof, took up residence, and began his first agricultural experiment—growing Smyrna tobacco.

The facilities erected for other station scientists were notably modest bungalows, perched high off the ground and adorned with neither porch nor stair landing. In 1902, the Territorial Legislature appropriated funds to build an office and a laboratory facility for a chemist at the Station, but because of subsequent budget cuts by the legislature, Edmund Shorey was not appointed as chemist until September 1903. Sugar was the principal agricultural industry in Hawaii, and soil, fertilizer, and entomological research already flourished at the privately funded Hawaiian Sugar Planters' Association Experiment Station.

Shorey, from the village of Lanark, Ontario, the son of a Methodist preacher, had been in the islands for nearly ten years. After taking the gold medal in chemistry as an undergraduate at Queen's University and the silver in natural sciences as a graduate student, he briefly contemplated the mining industry. Seeing few opportunities in Ontario, he moved to San Francisco and then to Hawaii, where he started work as a part-time sugar chemist. Among other projects, Shorey investigated microbiological and chemical conditions leading to loss of sucrose in raw cane sugar during prolonged transits from Hawaii to New York, around Cape Horn. The results of this important work were presented at the New York section meeting of the Society of Chemical Industry in May, 1898.[2] So satisfactory was Shorey's performance that he was placed in charge of operations at the largest sugar plant in the Kohala district.

Dr. Shorey accepted appointment as territorial food commissioner (the post to which Mr. Duncan succeeded) in 1900. In that position, he served as toxicologist (and probably microbiologist) in a large number of autopsies of persons who died without benefit of attending physician. His tenure as food commissioner was not entirely free of controversy. He was dead set against the practice of watering down milk, engaged in by some Hawaiian dairy farmers. Although the courts had ruled that a 10 percent dilution was permissible, Shorey continued to threaten exposure of the adulterators in the newspapers. Shortly before he resigned as food commissioner, the legislature passed Act 50, Sessions Law, 1903, setting the milk standards he had called for: no less than 11.5 percent total solids and 2.5 percent butterfat.

Shorey's real interest, however, was in the organic chemistry of soils. A job in the U.S. Department of Agriculture must have looked attractive, although when he started as chemist at the Experiment Station in 1903, there was little for him to do. His laboratory consisted in a room in the office building stocked with a few pieces of glassware and a Bunsen burner, a facility so inadequate that he continued to work in the food commissioner's laboratory (where Mrs. Stanford's toxicology was performed).

"The work done in this [the station's] laboratory was necessarily confined to such as could be done in small space with very simple apparatus," noted Special Agent Smith in his 1904 annual report.[3] Shorey's chemistry laboratory was not completed until October 1904. After a year of frustration, with little to occupy his time save collecting books for the library, he was ready to begin studies of nitrogenous compounds (including poisonous alkaloids) in Hawaiian soils. He was restless to engage in deeper analyses; to ask about nitrogen availability, not merely presence; and to take pleasure in the identification of new nitrogenous constituents—compounds like uvitonic and picolin carboxylic acids.[4] He would become known as a pioneer in this field.

It is likely that Smith, as the director of a station funded with public money (though inadequately, as is known),[5] required more immediately practical work of Shorey. Smith gave him tasks lacking challenge—analyzing samples of silk, inspecting foodstuffs for the army quartermaster, and certifying insecticides for private growers. In addition, as Shorey wrote in his annual report, "there [were] during the year quite a number of requests for analysis of soils and advice regarding fertilizers based on [that] analysis." He grumbled that "there is probably no more unsatisfactory task which can beset an analytical chemist than to give advice regarding the treatment of a soil based on chemical analysis only."

Experiment station, plantation, fertilizer, and private chemists have been working on them [soils] for years, and advice good, bad, and indifferent has been given. In consequence there are a large number of people here who consider chemical analyses of soils of no value whatever, and a perhaps equally large number who have implicit confidence in soil analysis to solve all the problems incident to the growing crops. This latter class is more difficult for the soil chemist to deal with, for if he refuses to give advice based on the examination of a handful of soil taken he knows not where or how, and about which he knows absolutely nothing except what is disclosed by the analysis, he is at once classed by them as incompetent.[6]

Given this revelation—that demands and expectations of chemists were unreasonable and criticism of their results the rule—it is not difficult to understand the uneasiness Shorey may have felt when he undertook the toxicological analysis of Mrs. Stanford's organs.

⌒ The "Ross Affair"

The reader requires an understanding of the "Ross affair" because the calamity that resulted led to serious tension in Mrs. Stanford's relationship with President Jordan. The affair caused her much pain, which she endured only through the support of friends and her faith in God's judgment. She could not rid her mind of it. The Ross affair was also the cardinal case in the later development of principles of academic freedom and tenure, although one historian has viewed it as, to some extent, "a freak."[1]

President Jordan had recruited Edward Ross to Stanford in 1893 to head the Department of Economics. He was twenty-six years old. In 1896, while teaching summer school at the University of Chicago, the student William Jennings Bryan Club had encouraged him to pen several articles on free silver for the *Chicago Record*, and these were compiled into a pamphlet, *Honest Dollars*. The author of the pamphlet was named as Edward A. Ross, professor of economics, Stanford University, and it was embellished with political cartoons and published by the Democratic National Committee for use in Bryan's presidential campaign. Ross enjoyed the notoriety; Mrs. Stanford found the pamphlet vulgar and was shocked that it bore her university's name.

That fall, Ross found himself in demand to speak on free silver at Bryan political rallies. He spoke at two, under the auspices of the National Silver League. Both speeches, Ross said, were nonpartisan, dispassionate, scholarly arguments against gold monometallism. Fortified by the tasteless campaign pamphlet and news clippings,[2] however, Mrs. Stanford advised President Jordan that, in her opinion, Professor Ross was not fit to be a department head at Stanford and should be dismissed.

After Jordan assured Mrs. Stanford of Ross's sound scholarship and outstanding teaching, as well as his concern that the professor's involuntary departure might bring unwanted publicity to the university, a compromise was reached. Jordan counseled Ross, informed him that his resignation would be requested were such transgressions to be repeated, and gave him the title of professor of sociology as a precaution. Ross accepted the terms: he liked Stanford University and wanted to remain. He was clearly pleased to be out of economics and into sociology, the field in which he was to make his reputation.[3]

On his return in 1899 from a sabbatical leave in Europe, Ross once again received invitations to give public lectures. It was Dr. Jordan, Ross later said, who recommended his participation at a labor meeting in San Francisco, to give the "scholar's view" on the Japanese immigration question that was so hotly debated. His presentation, as confirmed by Jordan's reading of the lecture notes, warned of population pressures: "I tried to show that, owing to its high, Malthusian birth-rate, the Orient is the land of 'cheap men' . . . scientifically coordinating the birth-rate with the intensity of the struggle for existence," as illustrated by the famines of overpopulated China and India.[4] And, Ross adds, "to quote one of the newspapers, [the lecture] 'made a profound impression.'"

It was the quotation from the *San Francisco Call* that made a profound impression on Mrs. Stanford the next morning. The *Call* reported that Professor Ross had rallied the crowd with, "And should the worst come to the worst it would be better for us to turn our guns on every vessel bringing Japanese to our shores rather than to permit them to land."[5] The next day she wrote Jordan that Ross's radical actions—his association with the evil elements of socialism, his intolerant "drawing [of] distinctions between man and man, all laborers and equal in the sight of God"—had brought her to tears. "I must confess I am weary of Professor Ross," she concluded, "and I think he ought not to be retained at Stanford University."[6]

It is thought that Jordan did not read the newspaper clipping but instead reiterated his respect for Ross, writing Mrs. Stanford that "He is . . . always loyal to what he thinks right . . . the best informed man on the Coast on matters of social and economic history . . . always very fair, always giving just treatment to both sides of every question."[7] Further exchanges, as well as a personal letter from Ross to Mrs. Stanford confirming his loyalty to her as the Mother of the university (she sent the letter to Jordan unanswered), did not sway Mrs. Stanford's opinion that Ross was a dangerous man and should be dismissed, although she agreed to a terminal year appointment were he to tender a letter of resignation at once.

Ross handed his letter to Jordan on June 5, 1900, the resignation to be effective at the end of the academic year, 1900–1901, at which point the president read him Mrs. Stanford's letter in which she had recommended his dismissal. Being neither a socialist nor a racist, as she had implied, Ross may have then decided that when the time came, he would make a public protest. When Jordan finally accepted his resignation on November 12, assuring him "once more [of] the high esteem in which your work as a student and a teacher, as well as your character as a man, is held by all your colleagues," Ross was ready with a response.

The next day, Ross presented the reporters of the campus newspaper with a full account of the events that culminated in his dismissal. It was a factual account containing nothing disrespectful of Mrs. Stanford or Dr. Jordan. "The scientist's business," Ross wrote, "is to know some things clear to the bottom, and if he hides what he knows, he loses his virtue." Jordan, unaware of Ross's press release, issued one of his own the same day. He praised Ross:

His discussions in the classroom are scientific and fair and have not, to my knowledge, been of such a nature as would tend to indoctrinate the students working with him. In his line of social science I consider him the most effective worker in the country. His character has always been unblemished and his reputation without a cloud.[8]

He was not "a martyr to freedom of speech," Jordan assured newsmen the following day after he had seen Ross's full statement. "I know that Mrs. Stanford's decision was reached only after long and earnest consideration and that its motive was the welfare of the University and that alone."[9]

Overwhelmingly, academicians, professional associations, and newspapers throughout the nation did not agree. To make matters worse, Professor Morton Aldrich resigned in protest that week, followed shortly by the popular and respected history professor, George Howard, and six others. But it was the adverse press coverage (particularly virulent from the San Joaquin Valley where Stanford's Southern Pacific Railroad was hated)[10] that had such a profound effect on Mrs. Stanford:

Have not matters reached a pretty state when a profound thinker like Professor Ross cannot freely express his convictions reached only after exhaustive research without being pulled down by the power of a wealthy but un-learned woman? —*Bakersfield Californian*

Professor Ross . . . has expressed opinions on economic subjects which do not please Mrs. Jane Stanford, who is not a scholar nor an economist, and whose opinion on the subjects discussed is of not the slightest importance to anybody. —*Fresno Republican*[11]

These insults—heaped upon an aging woman who had selflessly worked to build the splendid memorial to her son; followed scrupulously the plans she and Leland had laid down to serve the youth of California, of whatever class, means, or gender; abandoned her lifestyle and sold many of her jewels to fund the operating budget; and taken on the U.S. government in the Supreme Court and won—must surely have been felt most deeply when she read in Jordan's press release a quotation from her confidential letter to him: "My decision has not been the result of any hasty conclusion, but of disappointment, reflection and prayer."[12] As Bertha Berner recalls the occasion in Locarno, Switzerland, "When the storm broke she was . . . very unhappy and became ill and discouraged."[13]

As things stood in the public mind in mid November 1900, Ross had been fired by Mrs. Stanford in flagrant disregard of principles of academic freedom. Jordan, many thought, had yielded to the dictates of an "uncultured old woman." He ought to have resigned, they believed, in protest of Mrs. Stanford's dismissal of a professor he publicly avowed to be one of the best in the country. But as far as Mrs. Stanford was concerned, she had only *recommended* the dismissal, just as her husband had made recommendations to the president about faculty appointments. Under the terms of the founding grant, only the president of the university could discharge a member of the faculty. All Mrs. Stanford could do, in her capacity as surviving trustee, was discharge the president.

Mrs. Stanford wrote to Jordan from Rome on December 14: "I know that you thought Prof. Ross 'a consummate fool, a miracle of tactlessness,' but found 'that he was at bottom just a dime novel villain.' This really expressed your honest opinion, and it is time the world should know it."[14] She desperately wanted the university defended, as of course did Jordan.

In fact, his defense had begun long before, just two days after he had praised Ross to the newsmen. The president, who was understandably more than peeved that Ross had gone to the press, wrote a number of letters to disclaim his public characterization of Ross. Faculty members, alumni, and university presidents, were told now that Ross had a flawed character, his methods were "slangy and scurrilous," "appeal-[ing] to the poor against the rich," "an unsound, unscientific, impassioned appeal at a mass meeting led by professional agitators." He was "a dangerous man," as Mrs. Stanford had said all along.[15]

Jordan wrote to his friend Charles F. Lummis, editor of *The Land of Sunshine*:

> I have just learned what seems to me likely to be the real secret of Mrs. Stanford's feeling which is that . . . Dr. Ross used to condemn with a good deal of vigor in the classroom the means by which the wealth that entered into the university was acquired: that these attacks on Mr. Stanford's memory were brought to Mrs. Stanford's attention by students of Dr. Ross last year . . . Ross denies it entirely. This, of course, is not to be published but is furnished to you and any one to whom you wish to show it as a confidential statement of things as they look to me now.[16]

Lummis published the secret as quickly as he could. "The issue," he wrote in his December editorial, "is directly between Prof. Ross and Mrs. Stanford; and in this, fortunately, we need not depend on guess-work. . . . The precise words Prof. Ross may have used, I do not know. But I do know that he has said in his classes in Stanford many things which his students understood to be reflections on Senator Stanford."[17]

Jordan also wrote Ross that alumni had informed him of outrageous classroom remarks slandering Senator Stanford. Jordan added, "last year Mrs. Stanford was told this by a prominent alumnus, Mr. Croth-ers, if I understood correctly." But only the next day, Jordan wrote Ross again to say he had been hasty, that he had learned from Mr. Crothers that his understanding was incorrect.[18]

It is likely that Crothers had come to campus to inform Jordan that the San Francisco alumni had called an urgent meeting with the intent of drafting a statement supportive of Ross and critical of Mrs. Stanford's action. The alumni met at the YMCA to discuss how to deal with the crisis.[19] The debate among pro-Ross and pro-Stanford factions was so lengthy the group had to move to a vacant store on Mission Street after the YMCA closed, and it was concluded only when those needing streetcar or ferry transportation realized the last runs for the night were imminent. Fortunately for the university, the group agreed to appoint a committee of four to investigate the matter, and Crothers was placed on the committee. Not long after, at the annual meeting of the American Economic Association in Detroit, another committee was appointed with the same objective. Professor Edwin Seligman of Columbia University was named the chair.

While in Detroit, Ross heard rumors of President Jordan's letter-writing campaign. Alarmed, he wrote to Lester F. Ward, a distinguished sociologist, botanist, and geologist, as well as the uncle of his wife, Rosie, with whom he corresponded frequently about personal and professional matters. He was anxious to know whether Jordan was, "(as I hear) writing East letters which aim to justify Mrs. Stanford . . . that the scientific men were being flooded with letters of this sort. I am very anxious to find out *if* he is writing and just *what* he is writing." If Ward could find out about these "confidential letters" and their phraseology, he, Ross, could show Professor Seligman just what sort of a campaign was being waged.[20] Ward responded that he was not personally acquainted with anyone who had received a letter, but that if what he heard was true, and with respect to honor and morality, "no such scruples actuate your persecutors . . . we know he has written letters, especially to college presidents, etc., and if any of them can be got hold of by the committee, they will be good documents."[21]

The Stanford Alumni Report was finalized on January 26, 1901. It was brief, legalistic ("circular reasoning," reported the *Chronicle*), and completely exonerated Mrs. Stanford. It did not mention Jordan. Later Mrs. Stanford told George Crothers (who surely had a hand in writing the report) that without the support of the alumni, she "could not have borne the abuse of the Ross case."[22]

The Report of the Committee of Economists on the Dismissal of Professor Ross from Leland Stanford Junior University was issued on February 20, 1901. The committee's findings, not as clearly expressed as the alumni's, but nonetheless endorsed by fourteen leading academic economists, put the blame on Mrs. Stanford. The committee was also critical of President Jordan. When asked by the chairman to provide the facts of the case, Jordan had replied that Ross was simply not the proper man for the important post he occupied, that the matter was internal to Stanford. The committee concluded, "we cannot but feel that a refusal to furnish specific information in a case of such importance . . . is itself a fact of significance . . . much to be regretted."

Both reports were published in the March 8, 1901, issue of *Science* magazine, the official publication of the American Association for the Advancement of Science (of which Jordan was to become president in

1908). The *Science* editorial writer, calling attention to the opposite
conclusions of the reports, came down on the side of Stanford, arguing
that, in exercising his own freedom, Ross had ignored his obligation to
the university to protect her right to nonpartisanship. The editor also
quoted a paragraph from one of Ross's articles on Social Control that
he thought was illustrative of his radicalism. A more explicit attack on
Ross's writings appeared the following month in *Popular Science
Monthly*:[23]

his published writings and his lectures before his classes are extreme in their
rhetorical opposition to the wealth and conditions that made Stanford University possible. Thus, if we glance through his articles we find them strewn with
statements such as "the lawlessness, the insolence and the rapacity of private
interests"; "Under the ascendancy of the rich and leisured, property becomes
more sacred than person, moral standards vary with pecuniary status, and it is
felt that 'God will think twice before he damns a person of quality.'"

It seems extraordinary that an article containing these distortions,
little more than yellow journalism, should appear in a respected science
magazine. The quotations are from "Social Control. XVIII. The Radiant Points of Social Control," in which Ross discussed the historical
and psychological factors that allowed small social elements to exert a
large influence.[24] At the end of the science article, where the writer
twists Ross's lines from a second paper, using the provocative words
"parasitic organization . . . intimidate, beguile and cajole the exploited
majority," one wonders how he could have conceived that Ross had
used these words to describe his university teaching position when he
was, in fact, writing about medieval Europe.[25]

Ross saw the article in *Popular Science Monthly* and drafted a letter
of protest to the editor in which he pointed out that the articles quoted
referred to nobles and serfs and the caste societies of the Middle Ages.
On reflection, he knew his letter would be more likely published were
it submitted by Lester Ward, who enjoyed high standing in the scientific community. He sent Ward the draft and requested his opinion.
Ward advised Ross to drop the issue. "I presume I could get your protest printed," Ward wrote, "but it would be first submitted to Jordan
who would accompany it with an answer, using all his sophistry."
Ward did not think Ross would improve his case, but he added for reassurance, "The ichthyologists can't hurt you as long as the economists
are with you."[26]

In 1903, President Jordan prepared a paper entitled "The Ross Case,
by David Starr Jordan." Mrs. Stanford asked to read the manuscript.

She opined that it simply rehashed old events and assigned to her the responsibility for discharging Ross; she refused to have it published. Unknown to Jordan, she had prepared her own position paper on the case, which she intended to present to the Board of Trustees and, eventually, the public. She delivered her address, "On the Right of Free Speech," to the board on April 25, 1903. She reminded the board that the powers to appoint and dismiss faculty were exclusively in the hands of President Jordan. She pointed out that her opinion of Ross had been expressed more than four years before the president took action.

Meanwhile, Mrs. Stanford's intention to relinquish her administrative power to the Board of Trustees had come to the attention of Edward Ross, who was then on the faculty at the University of Nebraska. Ross saw the transfer as "tacitly confessing that a University can't be successfully run on a one-woman basis." As he wrote to Ward, the prospects for Stanford looked bright, and further that, "this action vindicates us [George Howard was also at Nebraska] and closes the episode."[27]

Not quite! In early fall, 1903, Ross received a copy of Mrs. Stanford's pamphlet "On The Right of Free Speech," to which she had appended Jordan's correspondence (including his letter characterizing Ross as a "consummate fool" and "dime-novel villain"). The "Stanford Case" now came into focus for Ross: although years earlier Mrs. Stanford had expressed her opinion that he was unfit for the job, it was Jordan who had actually fired him and then turned against him. It put the Stanford officials in a new light, as he quickly confided in a letter to Lester Ward, who was then abroad. About her published remarks, Ross wrote:

Mrs. Stanford displays honesty and frankness in spite of her conscientious intolerance[,] and I must say her address inspires in me a good deal of respect for her character. It will not hurt me but it will hurt Jordan terribly. The letters he wrote to her throughout the episode show him to be so cringing, shifty and mendacious that I don't see how he can ever regain his influence on the Pacific Coast. Some of my friends who have read the address think Mrs. Stanford's motive in giving out the whole correspondence is to make it impossible for Jordan to remain. Otherwise her action is inexplicable.[28]

⌒ Professor Julius Goebel

Professor Julius Goebel had been head of the German department for thirteen years when Jordan fired him. He was forty-eight years old. Several aspects of the Goebel case are of interest in relation to Mrs. Stanford's death—the timetable of Goebel's dismissal, the ludicrous charges Jordan concocted in both instances, and the resultant actions of the trustees to curb the president's power to dismiss faculty.

As Goebel's attorney, Mr. Denman, had briefed the *San Francisco Call* columnist, "it would seem that only Dr. Goebel's close relations with Mrs. Stanford prevented his removal before this time [spring 1905]."[1] Although Goebel might have overstated his friendship with Mrs. Stanford, it is clear from her letters to Horace Davis that she took his criticisms of the administration seriously. It seems unlikely that Jordan would have initiated actions against Mrs. Stanford's confidant during her lifetime unless some egregiously unprofessional or criminal act had been brought to his attention, which was not the case.

In *The Case of Julius Goebel*, Carnochan noted that the first evidence he could find showing Jordan's intentions was in a letter from George Crothers to Samuel Leib. Crothers reported that "about a month ago" Jordan had indicated he planned to dismiss Goebel "in the near future."[2] The letter was dated February 23, 1905. Whether Crothers informed Mrs. Stanford is not known. "About a month ago" would place the conversation in January, around the time Mrs. Stanford drank the poisoned Poland Spring water at Nob Hill.

There was no reason then to believe that Goebel's close relationship with Mrs. Stanford would soon come to an end. Before the poisoning (which did her health no harm) she had been engaged in an active New Year's social season in San Francisco, having recovered from an upper respiratory infection she had contracted in the East in December.[3] She was in good general health, had not needed to see her doctor for two years, and had it not been for pressing university duties, she might have been traveling in Europe. She had wanted to visit Bad Kissingen one last time, not for her health, but to renew memories of the pleasant times she and Leland had spent there together.[4]

Perhaps Mr. Denman overstated the dependency of Goebel's position on Mrs. Stanford. Perhaps Jordan was simply planning for the future.

The day after Mrs. Stanford's interment, President Jordan wrote to the Board of Trustees to request it terminate the chair of German occupied by Professor Goebel. He cited Goebel's lack of cordial relations and his meddling in the affairs of other faculty, and he enclosed a report from the university librarian showing that Goebel had failed to check out hundreds of books he had borrowed. The reader will recall that just the day before he had written to the Hawaii legislator Carl Smith to inform him of his moral certitude that Mrs. Stanford's bicarbonate of soda was spiked with strychnine after she died and to advise him to keep an eye on the hotel doctors. Surely, images of both Goebel and Mrs. Stanford were occupying Jordan's mind, pressing him to find innovative solutions—how to frame charges against Goebel on the one hand; how to explain Mrs. Stanford's death on the other.

The proceedings against Goebel were absurd, quite remarkably free of due process, consisting more in rumor and innuendo than factual charges that Goebel was deficient in his academic duties. Among the stated grounds for his dismissal: his ungentlemanly criticism of President Roosevelt's book *Winning of the West*; his upstaging the Music Department on an invitation to a German opera star to perform on campus; and his fraudulent report of a departmental meeting in which he gave the decision to stop teaching elementary German as a consensus when only he had voted in favor of the proposal. Goebel's later claim that his report was a simple error was likely to have been met with incredulity.[5]

Much of the notoriety of the case centered on Goebel's charge, well-covered in the newspapers, that Jordan had tried to bribe him. Facing certain dismissal, Goebel had applied for the one-year sabbatical leave to which he was entitled, while he sought another academic position. Jordan promptly responded that he would recommend the leave on receipt of Goebel's letter of resignation. The resignation was to be effective no later than July 31, 1906, but, Jordan warned, the arrangement might be terminated at any time "should conditions arise affecting the interests of the university which would make such action desirable." According to Goebel, the president's secretary, George Clark, made it clear to him that were he to go to the press, the salary would cease.

Goebel was livid: "Permit me to say in reply that you cannot buy my silence on any matter," whereupon Jordan fired him (on May 25, the day Welton Stanford offered a reward for apprehending his aunt's murderer), and Goebel released the letters to the newspapers, which did not hesitate to print them.[6]

To some of the trustees, it was another Ross affair—adverse press coverage, charges of despotic rule at Stanford, and threats of a boycott of faculty hiring by members of the Modern Language Association. Some trustees must have recalled that when George Howard had submitted his resignation to take place at the end of the academic year (he had not wanted to abandon his students), Jordan had accepted it on condition: his term would end sooner "should [Howard's] feelings in the matter prevent harmonious cooperation until that time." Howard was unwilling to "abide by the uncertain interpretation of the ambiguous phrase" and resigned at once.[7]

When Mrs. Stanford resigned her administrative powers in 1903, she appointed a Trustee's Committee on Organization. Much of the work of the committee was that of Horace Davis and George Crothers, who deliberated on the wisdom of having absolute power of removal of faculty in the hands of the president, as the founding grant required. Davis had long been uncomfortable with the provision. He had worried after the Ross firing (and, soon afterwards, that of another professor on "personal" grounds) that recruitment of faculty would be hindered by the absence of a fair and judicial process to safeguard their well-being.

Davis, now president of the board and personally involved in helping Goebel secure a job, sent a memorandum to board members urging that the president be persuaded to relinquish his power of removal to show that Stanford University stood for "intellectual freedom and individual liberty." Were Jordan willing, "this would be much the easiest way out of the difficulty," Davis argued.[8]

By December 27, 1905, when he received a copy of Davis's letter, Jordan realized that the board intended to give serious consideration to changing his absolute authority, a decision he said he would "cheerfully accept" provided the board did not suggest criticism of any past action he had taken.[9] One may wonder whether Davis's motion to reduce his authority provoked Jordan's thoughts of Mrs. Stanford's death and prompted the complex conspiracy theory reported in the newspapers on December 30, 1905.

On March 30, 1906, the Board of Trustees adopted a resolution, with Jordan's full approval, outlining the process for removal of a member of the faculty: presentation of a statement of charges; opportunity for the accused to present evidence to the standing faculty committee known as the Advisory Board; further review by the trustees as appropriate in an open session; and concurrence by a majority of the board.

The resolution was revealed to the academic world in an article in *Science* magazine entitled "Appointments and Removals at Stanford University,"[10] published in September 1906, coincidently three days before President Jordan asked the board to release the Ophüls report on Mrs. Stanford's autopsy. He may have been unable to free his mind of her death.

In 1907, Julius Goebel wrote to thank Horace Davis for his help in finding a position:

How did poor Mrs. Stanford . . . suffer, when it came to her knowledge, how this man, by his underhand methods, was shifting the entire blame for the Ross scandal on her shoulders, and how he was waiting for her death in order to be freed from his martyrdom."[11]

REFERENCE MATTER

⌒ Notes

Abbreviations

DPA	*Daily Palo Alto*
EB	*Evening Bulletin* (Honolulu)
HAES	Hawaii Agricultural Experiment Station
NYT	*New York Times*
PCA	*Pacific Commercial Advertiser* (Honolulu)
POP	*Paradise of the Pacific* (Honolulu)
SFC	*San Francisco Chronicle*
SFE	*San Francisco Examiner*
SUA	Stanford University Archives

Introduction

1. Stanford to Hopkins, Feb. 25, 1884, cited in Nagel, *Jane Stanford,* 22–23. Elliott reproduces the letter as reading *"really* at the highest point." *Really* strengthens the idea that the temperature had peaked. See Elliott, *Stanford University,* 11.

2. Ibid., 11–12. Many journalists concluded that the hallucination/dream was a spiritual visitation.

3. Ibid., 13.

4. Berner, *Mrs. Leland Stanford,* 34.

5. Ambrose, *Nothing Like It.*

6. Berner, *Mrs. Leland Stanford,* 14–15.

7. Ibid., 15.

8. C. Wenzel, "Finding Facts About the Stanfords in the California State Library" (address, California Historical Society, Sacramento, June 16, 1940), *California Historical Society Quarterly,* Sept. 1940.

9. Bain, *Empire,* 657.

10. G. M. Dodge, *Personal Recollections of President Abraham Lincoln, General Ulysses S. Grant and General William T. Sherman* (Council Bluffs, Iowa: Monarch Publishing, 1914), cited in Bain, *Empire,* 670.

11. After Senator Stanford died and while his will was in probate, the U.S.

government filed suit against the Stanford estate for repayment of bonds in
the amount of $15,237,000 that the government had issued the CPRR, based
on a California law that held individual stockholders liable in proportion to
shares owned for the debts and liabilities of corporations. The suit was dismissed by district and appeals courts but was taken by the solicitor general to
the U.S. Supreme Court. The brilliant Joseph Choate argued the case for Stanford, contending that the federal government had never intended individual li-
ability and that California law was not applicable. Justice John Marshall
Harlan agreed, writing that it was "unnecessary to consider any other question in the case." See *U.S. v. Stanford*, 161 U.S. 412 (1896). While litigation
was in progress, the probate court allowed Mrs. Stanford $10,000 per month
to cover her own expenses, as well as those of the university, on the grounds
that the professors were her "servants." She made many sacrifices but ended
up the winner.

12. Elliott, *Stanford University*, 9.

13. *San Francisco Examiner*, Apr. 17, 1889, cited in Elliott, *Stanford University*, 39.

14. Jordan, *Days of a Man*, 355.

15. Elliott, *Stanford University*, 25.

16. Moran, *David Starr Jordan*, 13.

17. Ager, *Four-Leaved Clover*, 91.

18. Jordan, *Life's Enthusiasms*, 54.

19. Jordan, *Story of a Good Woman*, 1. Jordan (M.D., Indiana University)
writes in a prefatory note: "She died in Honolulu, Hawaii, of a rupture of the
coronary artery," a diagnosis he offered on many occasions, which also appears in the annals of the Stanford Historical Society. See Bartholomew,
Brinegar and Nilan, *Chronology*, 40, but note the authors' caution: "The controversy about the cause of her death continues."

Jordan attributed the diagnosis to Dr. Ernest C. Waterhouse, whom he had
retained as a consultant. At least in his written reports, however, Waterhouse
never made such a diagnosis. Rupture of the coronary artery is exceptionally
rare, and the resulting hemopericardium and cardiac tamponade would have
been dramatically obvious to clinician and pathologist alike. Perhaps Jordan
referred to dislodgement, or "rupture," of an atheromatous plaque in the lu-
men of the coronary artery.

Chapter 1. The Death of Mrs. Stanford

1. Berner, *Mrs. Leland Stanford*, 204–5.

2. Corelli, *Mighty Atom*, 49.

3. Coroner's Inquest in re Death of Jane Lathrop Stanford, SUA. Except
where noted, inquest testimony cited is from this document.

4. *PCA*, Mar. 2, 1905.

5. *NYT*, Mar. 16, 1905.

6. Berner to Waterhouse, Mar. 14, 1905, SUA.

7. Waterhouse to Jordan, Mar. 14, 1905, SUA.

8. *NYT*, Mar. 16, 1905.

9. The Hawaii Attorney General's office was contacted to learn whether the Stanford University Libraries' copy of the coroner's inquest (marked Attorney General's Files, Case #361) was complete. The deputy attorney general responded that the documents could not be found and asked where Stanford had obtained its copy. The Stanford University archivist learned of the files from a paper presented by the archivist of Hawaii at the Archival Symposium, Berkeley, Calif., on Oct. 24, 1967, and promptly obtained a copy. Later, the files disappeared from the Hawaii State Archives.

10. Jordan to Leib, Mar. 22, 1905, SUA.

11. *DPA*, special ed., Mar. 1, 1905.

12. Jane L. Stanford autopsy report, SUA.

13. Strychnine and tetanus toxin produce the same neurophysiological effects on the spinal cord, but by different mechanisms. Both act to prevent the inhibitory action of the amino acid neurotransmitter, glycine. Strychnine blocks post-synaptic glycine receptors; tetanus toxin blocks pre-synaptic release of glycine from nerve terminals. Without glycine's regulation of reciprocal inhibition—of the triceps muscle, for example, when the biceps muscle contracts—both agonist and antagonist muscles contract simultaneously, resulting in the spasm that is so highly characteristic of either strychnine poisoning or clostridium tetani infection (tetanus).

14. Jordan later wrote to toxicologist Edmund Shorey, disclaiming strychnine poisoning: "The distortion of one limb mentioned by the two physicians was known to many of her intimate friends. . . . It was congenital and the same distortion appears in some other members of the same family." Such a preexisting condition, if present, could account for the asymmetry Wood noted when describing the distortion of *both* feet. See Jordan to Shorey, Apr. 13, 1905, SUA.

15. Simon and Swartz, "Anaerobic Infections," 10.

16. Finding cyanotic blood in both auricles suggests suffocation, not cardiac arrest. The heart continued to pump poorly oxygenated blood after respiration had ceased.

Chapter 2. The Poland Water Poisoning

1. *DPA*, Mar. 1, 1905.

2. *San Francisco Bulletin*, Feb. 19, 1905.

3. Crothers to Older, Jan. 30, 1947, SUA.

4. Stanford to Hopkins, Feb. 15, 1905, cited in Nagel, *Jane Stanford*, 171.

5. Poland Mineral Spring Water, a popular and agreeable water exceptionally low in mineral content, was bottled and shipped in Poland, Maine. The Stanford mansion stocked it by the case.

6. The poisonous alkaloids, strychnine and brucine, are found in commercial rodenticides prepared from the fruit seeds of the plant *Strychnos nux-vomica*. Brucine produces the same toxic effects but is much less potent than strychnine.

7. *SFC*, Mar. 4, 1905. The case of Dr. Warren was well known to toxicologists. He died accidentally after taking one-half grain of strychnine, having mistaken it for morphine to which he was addicted.

8. Dr. William Boericke, Mrs. Stanford's physician, was interviewed by a newsman concerning rumors that Boericke had dispensed medicinal jujubes to his patient whenever she offered a complaint. A report also circulated that Mrs. Stanford had put bicarbonate of soda in her Poland water, the soda perhaps being taken from the same bottle she took to Honolulu. The newsman wanted to know whether Dr. Boericke had prescribed the soda. He had not, he said, and, in fact, he had not seen her for two years before being called to consult on January 21, 1905. Boericke indicated that Mrs. Stanford rarely called upon his services except when she felt seriously ill. He had prescribed no jujubes to disguise the taste of any medicine.

Dr. Boericke, professor of homeopathy at the University of California, cofounder of the Pacific Homeopathic Medical College, and author of numerous texts on the Hahnemann theory of therapeutics, was a leading practitioner of homeopathy and is unlikely to have prescribed strychnine for Mrs. Stanford under any circumstances. Although Boericke considered nux vomica to be a polychrest—a helpful agent for thousands of symptoms—it was to him "preeminently a male remedy . . . for many of the conditions incident to modern life," for men who were "thin, spare, quick, active, nervous and irritable." Had he for some reason recommended it to Mrs. Stanford, the dose would have been homeopathic and harmless. See Boericke, *Pocket Manual*, 475.

9. Boessenecker, *Lawman*.

10. Teilhet and Boucher, "Demon in the Belfry."

11. *SFC*, Feb. 21, 1905.

12. *NYT*, Mar. 3, 1905.

Chapter 3. The Police Investigation

1. Bean, *Boss Ruef's San Francisco*, 42.

2. *SFC*, Mar. 3, 1905.

3. Spillane had just assumed the office of acting police chief. His predecessor, Chief George Wittman, was fired for complicity in a Chinese gambling protection scheme.

4. Callundan's appointment as captain of detectives had been promoted by the *San Francisco Examiner,* and the rival *San Francisco Call* had protested in an editorial on Jan. 13, 1900: "If Callundan be appointed chief of detectives San Francisco will be wide open to all the avenues that lead to corruption, degradation, vice, villainy, prostitution and crime." The *Call*'s ungrounded charges were soon to apply to the Schmitz/Ruef machine. See Boessenecker, *Lawman*, 290.

5. *DPA*, Mar. 2, 1905.

6. *San Francisco Call*, Mar. 8, 1905.

7. *SFC*, Mar. 4, 1905.

8. *San Francisco Call*, Mar. 8, 1905.

9. Fletcher, *Life and Career*; Barker, *Palmer*; Knott, *Trial*.

10. McLaren, *Prescription*.

11. *Atlanta News*, Mar. 14, 1905.

12. *PCA*, Mar. 11, 1905. Jordan's own sentiments on spiritualism were strongly tempered by his often-misguided eugenic beliefs. "Many of the 'psychic phenomena,'" he wrote, were "features of insanity. The phenomena of hysteria, faith cure, openness to suggestion, subjective imagery, mysticism, are not indications of spiritual strength, but of decay and disintegration of the nerves." See Jordan, *Heredity*, 143.

13. *San Francisco Call*, Mar. 5, 1905. The memorandum disclosed that the Stanfords had attended Mrs. Drake's séance six months after they had planned for the university in their wills. Jane Stanford added: "No spiritualistic influence affected the decision. Mrs. Drake had no more to do with it than a babe unborn" (Jordan, *Days of a Man*, 1: 365–66). For a fuller discussion of the Stanfords' spiritualism, see Tutorow, *Leland Stanford*, 228–31.

14. *PCA*, Mar. 11, 1905. Years after Jane Stanford's death, Thomas Welton Stanford, Leland Stanford's younger brother, gave Stanford University £10,000, the interest payout to be used for psychical research. The Department of Psychology was at first reluctant to administer the endowment because "the implications inherent in investigations in psychic or spiritualistic phenomena would give the undertaking a different character from that obtaining in ordinary cases of . . . scientific research." On receiving enthusiastic endorsement from other universities, however, the department established a Division of Psychical Research and named John Edgar Coover its first fellow. One of Coover's early experiments was to record pulse and respiration rates on a kymograph drum during the trances of a celebrated "trumpet" medium. As "trumpet" and "independent" voices floated through the darkened séance room of the California Psychical Research Society, where the experiments were conducted, Coover detected changes in the tracings that he attributed to movement of the psychic's vocal cords. Officers of the society did not agree with Coover's conclusion that the medium had subconsciously produced the ethereal voices. See Coover, *Experiments*, xix; Coover, "Investigation."

15. Stanford to Davis, Jan. 28, 1905, SUA. James—president of the Society for Psychical Research (London) in 1894–95 and founder of the American Society for Psychical Research—famously advocated psychical research. Quoting a scientific colleague, James wrote, "The great field for new discoveries is always the unclassified residuum." Despite evidence to the contrary, James always held that in the trance medium Mrs. Piper there was "a residuum of knowledge displayed that can only be called supernormal: the medium taps some source of information not open to ordinary people" (James, *Memories and Studies*, 200, cited in Coover, *Experiments*, 4). "If you wish to upset the law that all crows are black," James pointed out, "it is enough if you prove one single crow to be white. My own white crow is Mrs. Piper." He would have lent strong support to establishing a psychical research laboratory at Stanford—indeed, the "independent" voice in the sittings of Coover's trumpet medium was that of "Professor James." See James, *Will*, 319; Tanner, *Studies*.

16. *SFE*, Mar. 6, 1905. Edward Burns, Jordan's biographer, commenting on the negative reaction of the academic community to Jordan's firing of Professor Edward Ross, paraphrases a letter sent to Jordan: "Bitter aspersions were cast upon Jordan ... as a 'hired man' obeying the dictates of an 'uncultured old woman'" (Burns, *David Starr Jordan*, 17). The letter continued, "Can your self-respect endure it?" See Elliott, *Stanford University*, 354.

Chapter 4. The Honolulu Inquest

1. *DPA*, Mar. 3, 1905.
2. Hawaii Supreme Court Reports, 36: 794.
3. *PCA*, Mar. 7, 1905.
4. *San Francisco Call*, Mar. 7, 1905.
5. *PCA*, Mar. 7, 1905. The coroner's jury was so favorably impressed with Berner's testimony that it recommended her exoneration in its written verdict. Henry, in expunging the recommendation, explained to the jury that exoneration lay outside its authority (see *EB*, Mar. 13, 1905).
6. Ibid.
7. Tanner gives the usual autopsy findings in strychnine poisoning: "The hands are often clenched, and the soles of the feet are arched and inverted. The membranes of the brain and upper part of the spinal cord are congested. The lungs are loaded with dark fluid blood. The heart is usually contracted, but sometimes the right cavities are distended, like the pulmonary vessels, with black and liquid blood." See Tanner, *Memoranda*, 135–36.
8. Jordan to Leib, Mar. 22, 1905, SUA.
9. *PCA*, Mar. 3, 1905.
10. Inhomogeneity of an elixir containing strychnine caused the death of a woman who forgot to shake her bottle of tonic and as a result drank an excess of the chloroform layer, in which the strychnine was held in solution. See Blyth and Blyth, *Poisons, Their Effects and Detection*, 336.
11. Ibid., 346.
12. Ibid., 344.
13. Taylor, *On Poisons*, 50–51.
14. Ibid., 157.
15. Taylor was the forensic expert in the case of Dr. William Palmer of Rugeley, England, who, as mentioned earlier, was hanged for the murder of his gambling friend John Cook. Palmer complicated the forensic work by tampering with the evidence. He attended Cook's autopsy, where he jostled the prosecutor just as he opened the stomach, causing the gastric contents to spill into the peritoneal cavity. Taylor ordered a second autopsy to include abdominal viscera, but he was unable to isolate strychnine. Palmer was convicted on the basis of circumstantial evidence: he fraudulently collected Cook's racing winnings; he purchased strychnine; and he administered two pills to Cook, who shortly afterwards developed a tetanic spasm with generalized rigidity and cardio-pulmonary arrest. The mortuary assistant who laid out the body testified that she had prepared many corpses but had never seen

one as rigid as Cook's. It was revealed at his trial that Palmer had asked the Rugeley postmaster to intercept Taylor's report to the coroner. After reading of Taylor's failure to identify strychnine, Palmer wrote to the coroner, enclosing a £10 note and urging a verdict of "death by natural causes."

16. *San Francisco Bulletin*, Mar. 1, 1905.

17. *PCA*, Mar. 1, 1905.

18. *SFC*, Mar. 2, 1905.

19. Henry E. Highton was a prominent attorney, best known for his brilliant defense in the murder trial of Milton Kalloch, son of San Francisco Mayor Isaac Kalloch, whose remarkable gifts as a preacher had earned him appointment as pastor of the Tremont Temple in Boston at the age of twenty-three. Isaac Kalloch was a womanizer known as the "Sorrel Stallion." He had been tried for adultery in Boston but had avoided conviction when his attorney, Richard Henry Dana Jr., got a hung jury. Years later, Charles de Young, editor of the *San Francisco Chronicle*, bent on destroying Kalloch's political career, dug up the salacious story for the benefit of his subscribers. Kalloch countered with ungodly remarks from the pulpit about de Young's mother. Deeply offended, de Young shot Kalloch, hitting him in the chest and leg. Kalloch recovered, and de Young remained free on bail. When the editor persisted in exposing Kalloch, the latter's son Milton entered the *Chronicle* office on April 23, 1880, and shot Charles de Young, killing him in front of several witnesses. Dr. Jordan was visiting San Francisco for the first time and remembered the event in his memoirs.

Isaac Kalloch retained Henry Highton to defend Milton, and at the trial, Highton produced a witness, John Clementspaw, who was then serving time in San Quentin for perjury. He had given a false name at the de Young inquest, and his unsavoriness had been proven by the *San Francisco Call*'s discovery that he consorted with a convicted thief, Philomenia ("Galloping Cow") Faulkner. Clementspaw swore that de Young had fired first. Numerous prosecution witnesses swore, however, that de Young had not even drawn his pistol. One exuberant witness was certain that Kalloch had fired *six shots*, and it was on the basis of this testimony that Highton brilliantly argued his case: Milton's pistol was a *five-shooter*. Highton hoped, like Dana, for a divided jury. When the foreman read "Not Guilty," "Highton was so astonished he swallowed his tobacco cud." See Marberry, *Golden Voice*, 340.

Most believed de Young had got what he deserved. After Adolph Spreckels shot and wounded the *Chronicle*'s Michael de Young (Charles's brother) several years later, Ambrose Bierce quipped in the *Wasp*, "Hatred of de Young is the first and best test of a gentleman" (quoted in Brechin, *Imperial San Francisco*, 177). See also Bruce, *Gaudy Century*.

20. *San Francisco Call*, Mar. 8, 1905. The report is especially curious because on the previous day the *Call* columnist had written, "Attorney General Lorrin Andrews . . . apparently took no part in the proceedings." The questions were pertinent, but the outcome of the hearing would not have hinged on the answers. Something alerted Mrs. Stanford that she had been poisoned again, but whether she complained of a bitter taste is unclear. The inquest

stenographer's recording of Berner's statement is typographically ambiguous: "She never said anything about Jan'y happening made no remark of bitter taste on that night." If Andrews actually asked these questions, why were they expunged from the record? Coroner Rawlins, a young attorney with no experience in a case of this sort, may have ruled Lorrin Andrews out of order and struck his questions from the inquest transcript. But who censored kinsman Lorrin Andrews Thurston's *Pacific Commercial Advertiser*?

Chapter 5. The Stanford Party in Honolulu

1. *PCA*, Mar. 10, 1905.
2. *PCA*, Mar. 11, 1905.
3. *EB*, Mar. 14, 1905.
4. *San Francisco Call*, Dec. 31, 1905.
5. *PCA*, Oct. 23, 1903.
6. Decennial Record, Princeton.
7. Berner, *Mrs. Leland Stanford*, 153–54; Nagel, *Jane Stanford*, opposite 69. On the same page is a picture of Mrs. Stanford posing at the Sphinx with Berner, Richmond, and Beverly. The picture is enlarged in Nagel's second edition, *Iron Will*, with a caption "Jane Stanford and friends (Bertha Berner stands at left)" (142). Actually, Elizabeth Richmond stands at left, Berner is between her and Mrs. Stanford, and Beverly is sitting on the Sphinx.
8. Van Dine, in "Introduction," *HAES Press Bulletin*, no. 20, reproduced a letter from Cooper and Van Dine to Governor George Carter dated March 12, 1905. The letter refers to Dr. Jordan's mosquito fish experiment. The same letter may be found in the Stanford University Archives, dated Mar. 21, 1905. But in another letter, dated Mar. 23, 1905, Van Dine refers to his letter to the governor of Mar, 12, 1905. (See SUA, SC 58:1B, box 52, folder 268.) Jordan is said to have discussed Shorey's analysis of Mrs. Stanford's case with Van Dine; their meeting on or before March 12 seems likely. See Smith to Jordan, Dec. 27, 1906, SUA.
9. Jordan to Wilbur, May 18, 1921, SUA.
10. Testimony of Dr. Waterhouse, SUA.
11. Jordan told Mountford Wilson, "I asked him [Smith] to talk with Dr. Waterhouse and get his answers to two or three questions in regard to strychnine poisoning." See Jordan to Wilson, Apr. 13, 1905, SUA.
12. Waterhouse to Jordan, Mar. 14, 1905, SUA.
13. Gowers, *Manual*, 2: 1004–5.
14. Blyth and Blyth, *Poisons, Their Effects and Detection*, 340.
15. Delafield, *Handbook*, 6.
16. Berner told Callundan that Mrs. Stanford put her (Berner's) hands to her cheeks at the moment of death (*Call*, Mar. 22, 1905). In her memoir, Berner writes "she reached up and took my two hands and pulled them down around her neck" (Berner, *Mrs. Leland Stanford*, 207).
17. Waterhouse to Jordan, Apr. 5, 1905, SUA.
18. Berner to Waterhouse, Mar. 14, 1905, SUA.

19. Gowers, *Manual*, 2: 985.

20. Wilson, *Neurology*, 2: 793.

21. Taylor, *On Poisons*, 694.

22. Brundage, *Manual*, 176.

23. Blyth and Blyth, *Poisons, Their Effects and Detection*, 336.

24. Brundage, *Manual*, 177.

25. Taylor, *On Poisons*, 675.

26. Tanner, *Memoranda*, 135.

27. "The Treatment of Strychnine Poisoning," *Journal of the American Medical Association* 98 (1932): 1992–94.

28. Glycine also has inhibitory actions in the dorsal horns of the spinal cord where sensory networks are located. Here, the effect of strychnine blockade of glycine receptors is complex. For example, application of strychnine to the spinal cord of the cat results in an increased neuronal firing rate (that is, disinhibition) after the trivial sensory stimulus of deflecting a hair but not after the stimulus of pressure on the skin. Experiments of this kind help to explain the harmless effect of massaging Mrs. Stanford's limbs. See Sorkin and Puig, "Neuronal Model."

29. *NYT*, Mar. 15, 1905.

30. "The First Year at Stanford," 110. A biographical sketch prepared for Hawaii Supreme Court Reports, 43: 430, states that Smith was president of the student body and that Herbert Hoover was vice-president. This claim does not accord with Nash's finding that Hoover was class treasurer, but not until 1894. See Nash, *Herbert Hoover*, 10.

31. Smith to Jordan, Mar. 15, 1905, SUA.

32. Jordan to Smith, Mar. 28, 1905, SUA.

33. *EB*, Mar. 15, 1905; Jordan draft, misdated Mar. 16. 1905, SUA.

34. The *PCA* raised the possibility of hysteria on Mar. 11, 1905.

35. The permit to remove Mrs. Stanford's body from Honolulu was filed on Mar. 14, 1905, signed by Dr. Humphris, Mr. Pinkham of the Board of Health and D. P. Lawrence, registrar. The cause of death: "strychnine poisoning."

36. *Palo Alto Times*, special memorial ed., Mar. 24, 1905.

Chapter 6. The Stanford Party Returns Home

1. *San Francisco Call*, Mar. 22, 1905.

2. "Dr. Jordan has been assisting the detectives, to the extent of suggesting questions as a physician, during their inquiries regarding her symptoms and the results of the autopsy," the *San Francisco Call* reported on Mar. 15, 1905, but there is no evidence that Jordan participated in the interview of Humphris.

3. Berner to Waterhouse, Mar. 14, 1905, SUA.

4. *SFC*, Mar. 4, 1905. The pharmacist reported that Berner had asked him to wrap the bicarbonate of soda in paper, saying that they had a bottle to put it in at the house.

5. Jordan to Leib, Mar. 22, 1905, SUA. Jordan's characterization is all the more remarkable in that Dr. and Mrs. Humphris were prominent members of Honolulu society.

6. Jordan to Wilson, Mar. 22, 1905, SUA.

7. Jordan to Smith, Mar. 28, 1905, SUA. On arriving in San Francisco, Jordan told the press corps that Berner took *half* of the dose taken by Mrs. Stanford, detected no bitter taste, and suffered no ill effects. Later, Jordan wrote to Smith to explain his withdrawing the cablegram. After Mr. Kidd called the error to his attention, Jordan had questioned Miss Berner, who lowered the dose she purportedly took. There is no evidence, however, that Berner sampled the bicarbonate of soda at the same time as Mrs. Stanford. Berner testified at the inquest to taking soda in *early January*, but the soda had been replenished by February 28.

8. Jordan to Wilson, Mar. 23, 1905, SUA.

9. Jordan to Smith, Mar. 24, 1905, SUA.

10. Smith to Jordan, Mar. 15, 1905, SUA.

11. Humphris to Jordan, Mar. 20, 1905, SUA.

12. Jordan to Smith, Mar. 28, 1905, SUA; Jordan to Humphris, Mar. 28, 1905, SUA.

13. Humphris to Jordan, Apr. 11, 1905.

14. Shorey to Jordan, Mar. 31, 1905, SUA.

15. Jordan to Shorey, Apr. 13, 1905, SUA.

16. The *San Francisco Call*'s summary of Mar. 22, 1905, said Berner had removed the basin of water from Mrs. Stanford's lap. Jordan had already received a detailed addendum from Dr. Waterhouse in which he argued that too much emphasis had been given the pedal posture—"we know that the vessel *between Mrs. Stanford's feet* during the spasm just preceding death was not even overturned by any contraction [emphasis added]." See Waterhouse to Jordan, Apr. 5, 1905, SUA.

17. As mentioned earlier, the congenital distortion could account for the asymmetry of the strychnine-induced foot spasm detected at autopsy by Dr. Wood.

18. Smith to Jordan, Mar. 23, 1905, SUA. The evidence that Jordan obtained transcripts of the records is important in light of a claim that he had snatched the records from the police. In 1983, Stanford alumnus Stephen Requa made the acquaintance of Robert Van Dyke in Honolulu. After learning that Requa was a distant relative by marriage of Leland Stanford, Van Dyke, a local historian, told him he knew something about Mrs. Stanford's death. He claimed to have documentary evidence that President Jordan had played a role in her murder. Requa reported this information to a Stanford University administrator, but there was no follow-up, and Requa lost touch with Van Dyke.

In a telephone interview in 2002, Van Dyke told me that he had a large and unorganized collection of historical papers, documents, photographs, and books stored in a warehouse. It would be difficult for him to find the Stanford information, he said, but he remembered some of it clearly. He said that an elderly man had signed a statement, swearing that when he was a boy, a *man* in the Stanford party had sent him to the Benson-Smith drugstore, to fetch a prescription for Mrs. Stanford. Van Dyke had also been shown the journal of Dr. Nathaniel Emerson, a police surgeon and Honolulu historian, which was then in the possession of Dr. Emerson's son, Arthur. The journal had an entry about Mrs. Stanford's death, but the following seven pages had been torn out. Among Arthur's memorabilia was a letter from David Starr Jordan to his father, thanking him for his help in the case. Van Dyke gained the impression from Arthur that the surgeon had helped Jordan "spirit away" the police records. Van Dyke said he wrote a documentary film script, "Murder at the Moana." When he showed it to the San Francisco rare book dealer Warren Howell around 1970, Howell had asked, "Are you trying to blackmail Stanford?"

I could not find evidence to corroborate Van Dyke's unusual story. Both Arthur Emerson and Warren Howell are deceased. In 1996, Van Dyke sold much of his collection of Hawaiiana to the Bishop Estate in Honolulu. A Bishop librarian who worked for nine months to catalogue the material did not recall seeing any documents about Mrs. Stanford. An attorney hired to complete the inventory did not respond to a request for information. The Stanford University Archives contain no correspondence between Jordan and Nathaniel Emerson in 1905. The correspondence with Carl Smith refutes the claim Jordan "spirit[ed] away" the police records.

19. Waterhouse was variously described as "the best informed physician in Honolulu" (Jordan to Wilson, Apr. 13, 1905, SUA); "one of the best informed physicians of Honolulu" (Jordan to Humphris, Mar. 28, 1905, SUA); "the ablest physician we found available" (Jordan to Wilbur, May 18, 1921, SUA); "a well-informed physician" (Jordan, *Days*, 2: 156); "the only medical man in Honolulu who . . . would express an opinion in accordance with the views held by Dr. Jordan" (*San Francisco Call*, Sept. 7, 1905).

20. Jordan to Wilson, Apr. 13, 1905, SUA.

21. Smith to Jordan, Apr. 15, 1905, SUA; Waterhouse to Jordan, Apr. 23, 1905, SUA.

22. Jordan to Waterhouse, May 4, 1905, SUA.

23. Jordan to Wilson, May 10, 1905, SUA.

24. His fee of $350 in the case (equivalent to approximately $7,000 in 2001) may have jump-started Waterhouse's new career. In 1905, the annual rent for land in Pahang, Malaya, where he had his first plantation, was less than fifty U.S. cents an acre. His widowed mother was struggling financially to provide college educations for several younger children. Family legend has it that she economized by putting cardboard soles in her worn shoes. It seems unlikely that she would have been able to provide financial assistance to her son Ernest.

Chapter 7. Bolstering Dr. Jordan's Diagnosis

1. *San Francisco Call*, Mar. 10, 1905. Henry used the precedent of the "Botkin case" in referring the investigation to San Francisco. Cordelia Botkin

had mailed poisoned chocolates from San Francisco to Delaware in the successful murder of her lover's estranged wife. The courts ruled that prosecutorial jurisdiction resided in California, not Delaware, and District Attorney Byington tried the case. Sensational reporting by the crack *Examiner* newswoman Lizzie Livernash, circumstantial evidence, and leading instructions to the jury by Judge Carroll Cook led to a verdict of guilty and a life sentence. Because of Cook's prejudicial handoff, Cordelia was retried just a few months before Mrs. Stanford's death. It was only just. A retrial had also been granted Albert Frederick George Vereneseneckockockhoff (known as "Hoff") after Judge Carroll had instructed his jury that "circumstantial evidence has this great advantage; that various circumstances from various sources are not likely to be fabricated." One of the circumstances weighing against Botkin was testimony that she asked her doctor, "By the way, if a person wanted to commit suicide, what would be the best thing to take? How would it be to use strychnine?" Strychnine would be severe, the doctor advised; arsenic would be milder. See Offord, "Gifts of Cordelia," 137–38.

2. Within two years, Dinan would be indicted for conspiring with Ruef to protect a popular brothel at 712 Pacific Street. Dinan was arrested, posted bail, and continued as police chief.

3. *SFE*, May 26, 1905.

4. *NYT*, Dec. 31, 1905.

5. Berner, *Mrs. Leland Stanford*, 209–10.

6. Berner, *Incidents*, 182, SUA.

7. Nagel, *Jane Stanford*, 174.

8. Boessenecker, *Lawman*, 306.

9. Babcock, *Diseases*, 518.

10. Ophüls, *Arteriosclerosis*, 54.

11. Ibid., 96

12. Carnochan, "Case of Julius Goebel." Stanford Registrar Orrin Elliott gives the timing of Jordan's key actions against "a professor," curiously never revealing Goebel's name:

> February 25, 1905 (three days before Mrs. Stanford's death)—Jordan warns Goebel, "The value of your services . . . is notably impaired";
> March 25, 1905 (the day after Mrs. Stanford's funeral)—Jordan asks trustees to abolish Goebel's professorship;
> May 25, 1905 (the day Stanford officials report no poison found in Mrs. Stanford's organs)—Jordan notifies Goebel of his summary removal.

See Elliott, *Stanford University*, 487–88.

13. *Hawaiian Star*, Aug. 23, 1905.

14. Bartholomew, "Mystery." A granddaughter of Waterhouse's living in Honolulu, whose father was a cardiologist, knew little of Mrs. Stanford's death until reading Bartholomew's article, sent to her from Nashville, Tennessee.

15. *San Francisco Call*, Sept. 7, 1905.

16. *San Francisco Call*, Jan. 4, 1906.

17. Jordan to Otaki, Apr. 13, 1905, SUA. Otaki was a Japanese ichthyologist who had attended Stanford University, where, as an undergraduate, he had served as the Jordan household cook to help make ends meet. See Jordan, *Days of a Man*, 2: 10.

18. *PCA*, Jan. 3, 1906.

19. *PCA*, Jan. 4, 1906.

20. Humphris to Jordan, Jan. 15, 1906, SUA.

21. Jordan to Humphris, Jan. 27, 1906, SUA.

22. Humphris to Jordan, Feb. 10, 1906, SUA.

23. Jordan to Humphris, Feb. 24, 1906. SUA.

24. *San Francisco Call*, Dec. 31, 1905.

25. Jordan to Wilbur, May 18, 1921, SUA.

26. Jordan to Board of Trustees, Sept. 24, 1906, SUA.

27. Mirrielees, *Stanford*, 113. Mirrielees was unable to discover the identity of the individual (Goebel) who had listed the weak departments for Mrs. Stanford. "Certainly not the President," she writes. Horace Davis, George Crothers, Timothy Hopkins? "Whoever he was, the reasons that guided his selections are as hard to find as his name."

Chapter 8. The Cases of Shorey and Humphris

1. Smith to Jordan, Dec. 27, 1906, SUA.

2. Smith to Jordan, Nov. 22, 1905, SUA.

3. Smith to Jordan, Dec. 27, 1906, SUA.

4. Jordan to Smith, Jan. 8, 1907, SUA.

5. Smith to Jordan, Jan. 28, 1907, SUA.

6. Jordan to Smith Feb. 6, 1907, SUA.

7. Report of the President, 26.

8. Jordan to Wilbur, May 18, 1921, SUA.

9. Jordan to Leib, Mar. 22, 1905, SUA. Jordan's calculation of "one part in 1324" is slightly off. Using the average of the three analyses of strychnine, one part in 1,357 is correct.

10. Smith and Blacow, *HAES Press Bulletin*, no. 12 (1905). The authors credit Shorey with the analyses. The bulletin discusses the success of the experimental tobacco farm Smith started at the station, the first serious attempt to grow tobacco in Hawaii. Smith later took advantage of the government-sponsored research (one wonders whether Shorey perceived a conflict of interest). He was honored at a University Club dinner "to signal his enlistment in the band of small farmers . . . having resigned his position as Special Agent in Charge of Hawaii Experiment Station to engage in tobacco culture for his personal interests." *POP* 21 (1908): 9.

11. W. P. Kelley and William McGeorge, *HAES Press Bulletin*, no. 34 (1912).

12. Smith, *HAES Annual Report*, 1907.

13. Queen's University *Review*, 1934.

14. Jordan to Wilbur, May 18, 1921, SUA.

15. Humphris, *Artificial Sunlight,* dedication.
16. Ibid., x–xi.
17. Humphris, "Presidential Address."
18. *British Medical Journal,* obituary of F. Howard Humphris, F.R.C.P. June 28, 1947, 951–52.
19. Humphris, "What Is Pain?" 1906.
20. Ibid., 108. It is of interest to note that when Humphris read the same paper a year later at the American Electro-Therapeutic Association meeting in Boston, his distinguished mentor Dr. Snow remarked, "Personally, I want to thank Dr. Humphris for his excellent paper. It is a view that I have long had in my own mind, although I am certain that I could not have expressed it as clearly as he had." See Humphris, "What Is Pain?" 1908.
21. Katsuki, "Suggestion."
22. Dr. James Judd, Dr. Waterhouse's partner, nominated Humphris for office.
23. Humphris, Hawaiian Territorial Medical Society minutes, 1909.
24. Catts, "Medical Society."
25. Humphris, "On Ascertaining the Depth."
26. Humphris, "Melted Paraffin."
27. Humphris, "Light and Its Therapeutics," 23–24.
28. Humphris, "Light in the Prevention of Rickets," 266. Humphris's approach to prevention contrasted sharply with that of David Starr Jordan, who wrote contemporaneously on another congenital deficiency disease—cretinism, caused by lack of iodine. Clinging to strongly held eugenic principles of "betterment," even after iodine administration to pregnant women had been proven to prevent cretinism, Jordan reiterated his long-held sentiments about these unfortunate children: "awful paupers—human beings with less intelligence than the goose, with less decency than the pig." The remedy, Jordan was certain, lay in segregation of cretins to prevent breeding, "the guarantee that each individual shall be the last of his generation." See Jordan, *Days of a Man,* 2: 314–15.
29. Dr. Waterhouse died three months later, under much different circumstances.
30. Humphris, "Electricity in the Relief of Pain."

Chapter 9. The Other Physicians

1. *British Medical Journal,* obituary of F. Howard Humphris. Humphris, a master chef, fond of the luau in his Honolulu days, was also remembered for his cocktails—"puzzling in their makeup, with spices from the plains of Arabia, curious and exotic fruits from the shores of Honolulu . . . baffling in character . . . potent beyond words." See also Humphris, "Feasting."
2. *PCA,* June 2, 1906.
3. Pratt, *Hawaii,* 16.
4. Jordan to Leib, Mar. 22, 1905, SUA.
5. *Hawaiian Star,* Aug. 23, 1905.

6. *PCA*, Apr. 20, 1900.

7. Katsuki, "Medical Men."

8. *Three Years After.*

9. *PCA*, Aug. 28, 1905.

10. Isenberg, *Early Memories*, 7. Perhaps the naming idea came from Thomas Pinder's employee John Kipling, who a few years earlier had wooed his wife, Alice, at Lake Rudyard.

11. Siddall, *Men of Hawaii*, 409.

12. Annual Report of the Honolulu Chamber of Commerce, 1910 and 1911. Exports of rubber from Malaya rose threefold between 1908 and 1910, largely because of Henry Ford's introduction of assembly-line production of cars. See Drabble, *Rubber*, 62.

13. Wilson, *With All Her Might*, 79.

14. Ibid., 82.

15. Humphris, "Anterior Poliomyelitis."

16. *PCA*, Feb. 16, 1923.

17. *Honolulu Star Bulletin*, Feb. 17, 1923.

Chapter 10. Perpetuating the Myth

1. Burns, *David Starr Jordan*, 22.

2. Jordan, *Days of a Man*, 1: vii.

3. Elliott, *Stanford University*, 464. Elliott refers the reader only to pages 203–7 of Berner's book, *Mrs. Leland Stanford*. These pages recount the events of February 28, 1905, through Mrs. Stanford's death. It is on pages 208–10 that Miss Berner gives the details of the investigation and the Ophüls report.

4. Berner, *Mrs. Leland Stanford*, 207.

5. Mirrielees, *Stanford*, 115. In the Berner memoir, accidental drinking of cleaning solution was a "belief entertained" but was not given as a *final* determination.

6. Crothers to Older, Jan. 30, 1947, SUA. Crothers wrote that Mrs. Stanford told him that after she had drunk the Poland water, she telephoned President Jordan to ask him "what was the bitterest thing in the world?" Jordan said he first learned of the episode when he met Mrs. Stanford and Miss Berner on a streetcar the following morning. See Jordan to Wilbur, May 18, 1921, SUA.

7. Stanford to Crothers, Feb. 15, 1905, cited in Nagel, *Jane Stanford*, 170.

8. Crothers to Older, Jan. 30, 1947, SUA.

9. Older, *San Francisco*, 54.

10. Clausen, *Stanford's Judge Crothers*, 67.

11. Nagel, *Jane Stanford*, 174.

12. "Stanford News," Stanford University News Service, Apr. 2, 1986.

13. Spoehr, "Progress' Pilgrim," 138.

14. Ogle, "Mysterious Death"; Casabona, "Suspicious Death"; Boessenecker, *Lawman*. Casabona's account was published in three installments in the student newspaper when she was a freshman at Stanford. She reported

Jordan's efforts to cover up Mrs. Stanford's poisoning, discussed the suicide theory, and concluded, "This writer, for one, does not believe Mrs. Stanford died from munching on too much gingerbread and chocolate." Her story raised eyebrows on campus, provoking discussions in classrooms and at coffee tables in the student union. "Some people loved it, others made fun of it, but everyone read it," Helen Casabona remembers (personal communication).

Chapter 11. Summing Up

1. Some historians point out that in 1905, strychnine was commonly included in compounded medicines, "including Mrs. Stanford's prescription." The latter conclusion, however, is not supported by the evidence. See Bartholomew, Brinegar, and Nilan, *Chronology*, 40.

2. Waterhouse to Jordan, Apr. 5, 1905, SUA.

3. Jordan to Shorey, Apr. 13, 1905, SUA.

4. Crothers to Older, Jan. 30, 1947, SUA.

5. Jordan to Leib, Mar. 22, 1905, SUA.

6. Jordan to Shorey, Apr. 13, 1905, SUA.

7. Spoehr, "Progress' Pilgrim," 216.

8. Jordan to Board of Trustees, Sept. 24, 1906, SUA.

9. President Jordan's motto was "Die Luft der Freiheit weht" ("The wind of freedom blows").

10. Eliot to Jordan, Oct. 31, 1905, cited in Elliott, *Stanford University*, 490.

11. Carnochan, "Case of Julius Goebel."

12. *San Francisco Call*, June 2, 1905.

13. *SFC*, June 2, 1905.

14. Goebel to Stanford, June 6, 1904, cited in Carnochan, "Case of Julius Goebel."

15. Stanford to Davis, July 14, 1904, SUA.

16. "Stanford Hazards Escaped." Notes of G. E. Crothers, Mar. 23, 1932, in Orrin L. Elliott papers, SUA.

17. Crothers to Leib, Feb. 23, 1905, cited in Spoehr, "Progress' Pilgrim," 187.

18. Ibid., 138.

19. Jordan, *Days of a Man*, 2: 156.

Appendix 1. Dr. Shorey and the Experiment Station

1. The announcement in Honolulu of Smith's appointment by the U.S. Department of Agriculture was read by some as implying native Hawaiians were primitive barbarians. "Mr. Smith's advent on these shores was not noted with those feelings of distinguished consideration usually exhibited upon the appearance of Federal officials," wrote the *Paradise of the Pacific* in July 1901. It was a misunderstanding. Smith was readily accepted and later honored for his work. See *POP* 21 (1908): 9.

2. Shorey, "Deterioration." Presiding at the session was Dr. Charles F.

Chandler, Columbia professor of analytical chemistry, whose favorable mineral analysis of Poland Spring water for Hiram Ricker & Sons had helped launch its worldwide distribution. Falkenau's analysis of the poisoned water showed an amount of solid material greatly in excess of Chandler's original measurement.

3. Smith, *HAES Annual Report*, 1904, 362.
4. Shorey, "Organic Nitrogen."
5. Crawford, "Hawaii's Position."
6. Shorey, *HAES Annual Report*, 1904, 371.

Appendix 2. The "Ross Affair"

1. Furner points out that the Ross case was not representative, because only at Stanford did the power to dismiss a faculty member rest in the hands of a single trustee. Her point about autocracy is well taken, but it is helpful to an understanding of the interpersonal dynamics of the case to know that the power was in the hands of President Jordan, *not* of Mrs. Stanford. See Furner, *Advocacy*, 256. See also Elliott, *Stanford University*, 326–78; Nagel, *Jane Stanford*, 134–46; Metzger, *Academic Freedom*, 162–71; Mohr, "Academic Turmoil"; Ross, *Seventy Years*, 64–86. Although historians generally refer to the affair as the "Ross Case," Ross preferred the "Stanford Case."

2. Years later, Mrs. Stanford mentioned that her poor opinion of Ross preceded the Bryan rallies. She was doubtless aware of the scathing attack on the university (and her husband) by the *Portland Oregonian* after Ross gave an extension course in that city in the summer of 1895. Describing Ross's monetary positions as "harmless enough but for the factitious authority given them by the pretense of university teaching," the editor concluded:

> If anything were lacking to hasten the downfall of this plutocratic establishment, founded on the pride of up-start wealth obtained through robbery, the want would be supplied through the lectures of peripatetic professors who show and prove by their treatment of economic and moral questions that they are true to the instinct and practice on which their establishment was founded.

See Ross, *Seventy Years*, 61–62.

3. Ross's longtime colleague J. L. Gillin commented years later, "In some ways he might be called not inappropriately the Abraham Lincoln of American sociology." See Gillin, "Personality," 542.
4. Ross, *Seventy Years*, 70.
5. *San Francisco Call*, May 8, 1900.
6. Stanford to Jordan, May 9, 1900, cited in Elliott, *Stanford University*, 341.
7. Jordan to Stanford, May 11, 1900, cited in Elliott, *Stanford University*, 342.
8. The Ross and Jordan press releases of Nov. 14, 1900, are to be found in Ross, *Seventy Years*, 69–72.

9. Elliott, *Stanford University*, 356.

10. See Norris, *Octopus*.

11. Mohr found some 2,000 newspaper clippings on the Ross affair in the Stanford University Archives, almost all of which were critical of Mrs. Stanford. See Mohr, "Academic Turmoil," 49–52.

12. Stanford to Jordan, May 23, 1900, cited in Elliott, *Stanford University*, 347.

13. Berner, *Mrs. Leland Stanford*, 137.

14. Stanford to Jordan, Dec. 14, 1900, cited in Nagel, *Jane Stanford*, 137.

15. Elliott, *Stanford University*, 359–60.

16. Jordan to Lummis, Nov. 18, 1900, SUA.

17. Lummis, *Land*, 447.

18. "The Case of Professor Ross," 366. Ross was later to show these letters to a committee of the American Economic Association appointed to investigate the facts of his dismissal. In its report, the committee quoted Ross as testifying, "I have never referred in a derogatory way to Senator Stanford, nor have I reflected on the manner in which he accumulated his fortune." Jordan's (and others') statements were "a thorough-paced falsehood and a disingenuous attempt to befog the real issue."

19. Crothers's notes of the meeting are in "Stanford Hazards Escaped," Orrin L. Elliott papers, SUA.

20. Ross to Ward, Jan. 9, 1901, cited in Stern, "Ward-Ross II," 744.

21. Ward to Ross, Feb. 3, 1901, ibid., 744–45. Ward was sufficiently outraged to have heard rumors of what he considered slanderous charges against Ross that he advised: "Perhaps the committee can secure a few [letters], or even a refusal to send them would be useful information."

22. Crothers, "Stanford Hazards Escaped," Orrin L. Elliott papers, SUA.

23. Both *Science* and *Popular Science Monthly* were under the editorship of James McKeen Cattell.

24. Ross, "Social Control XVIII," 245–46. Had the science writer carefully read the article, he might have noted an earlier paragraph: "When the moneyed man holds the baton in the social orchestra, the keynotes will be industry, thrift, providence, sobriety, probity, civility, the peaceable demeanor, and the keeping of engagements." The keynotes matched Mrs. Stanford's ethical values exactly.

25. Ross, "Social Control. XIX," 388. Ross published a series of twenty articles that became the basis for his well-received book *Social Control*, published in 1901. Lester Ward rated it most favorably: "probably the most important contribution thus far made to the genesis and essential nature of social order . . . sparkl[ing] with happy phrases, quaint words and pat illustrations." See Ward, "Contemporary Sociology," 758.

26. Ward to Ross, Apr. 24, 1901, cited in Stern, "Ward-Ross II," 746.

27. Ross to Ward, Mar. 14, 1903, cited in Stern, "Ward-Ross III," 708. Ross frequently worried that colleagues who had resigned to protest his firing, particularly George Howard, would suffer permanent damage to their careers.

He was not relieved of this anxiety until Howard received an appointment at the University of Chicago.

28. Ross to Ward, Sept. 13, 1903, cited in Stern, "Ward-Ross III," 716.

Appendix 3. Professor Julius Goebel

1. *San Francisco Call,* June 2, 1905.

2. Crothers to Leib, Feb. 23, 1905, cited in Carnochan, "Case of Julius Goebel."

3. Berner, *Mrs. Leland Stanford,* 196–97. In December 1904, Mrs. Stanford visited cousins in Norwich, Connecticut, staying late into the evening while Berner modeled antique gowns. Mrs. Stanford had walked back to her hotel in very cold, snowy weather.

4. Stanford to Miller, September 10, 1904, SUA.

5. Goebel said he had taken the department secretary's notebook, containing the minutes of the meeting, to his home to work on the report. The minutes had been lost when one of his children had torn the pages out of the notebook, and he had relied on his memory to write the report. He also blamed his failure to check out library books on simple absentmindedness. See *SFC,* June 2, 1905.

6. *San Francisco Call,* June 2, 1905.

7. "Leland Stanford Junior University," 143.

8. Davis to Grant, December 18, 1905, cited in Spoehr, "Progress' Pilgrim," 204; Elliott, *Stanford University,* 490.

9. Jordan to Grant, January 20, 1906, cited in Elliott, *Stanford University,* 491.

10. "Appointments and Removals," 380–81. Although the *Science* article was entitled "Appointments and Removals at Stanford University," the text of the board's resolution was confined to the removal process. The editor credited the text to Jordan's annual report to the Board of Trustees.

11. Goebel to Davis, July 25, 1907, cited in Carnochan, "Case of Julius Goebel."

☞ Select Bibliography

Ager, Carolus [Charles Kellogg Field]. *Four-Leaved Clover*. San Francisco: C. A. Murdock, 1899.

Ambrose, S. E. *Nothing Like It in the World: The Men Who Built the Transcontinental Railroad, 1863–1869*. New York: Simon & Schuster, 2000.

Annual Report of the Honolulu Chamber of Commerce for the year ending August 16th, 1910. Honolulu: Hawaiian Gazette Co., 1910.

Annual Report of the Honolulu Chamber of Commerce for the year ending August 16th, 1911. Honolulu: Hawaiian Gazette Co., 1911.

"Appointments and Removals at Stanford University." *Science*, n.s., 24 (1906): 380–81.

Arnold, H. L., Jr. "Hawaii Medical Association, 1856–1956." *Hawaii Medical Journal* 15 (1956): 313–24.

Babcock, R. H. *Diseases of the Heart and Arterial System*. New York: D. Appleton, 1903.

Bain, D. H. *Empire Express: Building the First Transcontinental Railroad*. New York: Penguin Books, 2000.

Barker, Dudley. *Palmer, the Rugeley Poisoner*. London: Duckworth, 1935.

Bartholomew, Karen. "The Mystery of Jane Lathrop Stanford's Death." *Stanford Observer*, June 1991, 24.

Bartholomew, K., C. Brinegar, and R. Nilan. *A Chronology of Stanford University and Its Founders, 1824–2000*. Stanford: Stanford Historical Society, 2001.

Bean, Walton. *Boss Ruef's San Francisco: The Story of the Union Labor Party, Big Business, and the Graft Prosecution*. 1952. Reprint. Berkeley: University of California Press, 1967.

Berner, Bertha. *Incidents in the Life of Mrs. Leland Stanford, by Her Private Secretary, Bertha Berner*. Ann Arbor, Mich.: Edwards Brothers, 1934.

———. *Mrs. Leland Stanford: An Intimate Account*. Stanford: Stanford University Press, 1935.

Blyth, A. W., and M. W. Blyth. *Poisons, Their Effects and Detection*. 1884. 4th ed. rev. London: C. Griffin and Co., 1906.

Boericke, William. *Pocket Manual of Homœopathic Materia Medica: Com-*

prising the Characteristic and Guiding Symptoms of All Remedies (Clinical and Pathogenetic). 9th ed. New York: Boericke & Runyon, 1927.

Boessenecker, John. *Lawman: The Life and Times of Harry Morse, 1835–1912.* Norman: University of Oklahoma Press, 1998.

Brechin, Gray. *Imperial San Francisco: Urban Power, Earthly Ruin.* Berkeley: University of California Press, 1999.

British Medical Journal. Obituary of F. Howard Humphris, F.R.C.P. June 28, 1947, 951–52.

Bruce, J. R. *Gaudy Century: The Story of San Francisco's Hundred Years of Robust Journalism.* New York: Random House, 1948.

Brundage, A. H. *A Manual of Toxicology: A Concise Presentation of the Principal Poisons with Detailed Directions for the Treatment of Poisoning, Also a Table of Principal and Many New Remedies.* 7th ed. New York: H. Harrison, 1909.

Burns, Edward McNall. *David Starr Jordan: Prophet of Freedom.* Stanford: Stanford University Press, 1953.

Carnochan, W. B. "The Case of Julius Goebel: Stanford, 1905." *American Scholar* 72 (2003): 95–108.

Casabona, Helen. "Jane Stanford's Suspicious Death in Hawaii." *Stanford Daily*, November 4–6, 1981.

"The Case of Professor Ross." *Science* 13 (1901): 361–70.

Cassity, Turner. "Mrs. Leland Stanford," From "Imaginary Sargents" in *The Destructive Element: New and Selected Poems.* Athens: Ohio University Press, 1998.

Catts, A. B. "Medical Society in the Early 1900s." *Hawaii Medical Journal* 54 (1995): 776–79.

Clausen, H. C. *Stanford's Judge Crothers: The Life Story of George E. Crothers. Faithful Son; Loyal Citizen and Political Leader; Successful Lawyer, Jurist, and Businessman; Wise Counselor and Kindly Benefactor.* San Francisco: George E. Crothers Trust, 1967.

Cooke, S. J. *Sincerely, Sophie.* Honolulu: Tongg Publishing, 1964.

Coover, J. E. "Investigation with a 'Trumpet' Medium." *Proceedings of the American Society for Psychical Research* 8 (1914): 201–52.

———. *Experiments in Psychical Research.* Stanford: Stanford University, 1917.

Corelli, Marie. *The Mighty Atom.* Philadelphia: J. B. Lippincott, 1896. Reprint. London: Sphere Books, 1975.

Coroner's Inquest in re Death of Jane Lathrop Stanford. SUA.

Crawford, D. L. "Hawaii's Position in Experiment Station Appropriations." *University of Hawaii Occasional Papers,* No. 6. Honolulu: University of Hawaii, 1927.

Decennial Record of the Class of Eighteen Hundred and Ninety-four, Princeton University. N.p., June 1904.

Decennial Record of the Class of 1898, College of Physicians and Surgeons, Columbia University in the City of New York. Decennial Reunion. N.p., March 7, 1908.

Delafield, F., and T. M. Prudden. *A Handbook of Pathological Anatomy and Histology.* 7th ed. New York: William Wood, 1904.

Drabble, J. H. *Rubber in Malaya, 1876–1922: The Genesis of the Industry.* Kuala Lumpur: Oxford University Press, 1973.

Eckart, C. F. "Work of the Experiment Station and Laboratories of the Hawaiian Sugar Planters' Association." Honolulu: Hawaiian Gazette Co., 1902.

———."Miscellaneous Papers." Report of Work of the Experiment Station of the Hawaiian Sugar Planters' Association. *Division of Agriculture and Chemistry Special Bulletin B.* Honolulu: 1905.

Elliott, O. L. *Stanford University: The First Twenty-five Years.* Stanford: Stanford University Press, 1937.

Felter, H. W., and J. U. Lloyd. *King's American Dispensatory.* 18th ed. Cincinnati: Ohio Valley Co., 1898.

"The First Year at Stanford: Sketches of Pioneer Days at Leland Stanford Junior University." 2d ed. Stanford University English Club, 1910.

Fletcher, George. *The Life and Career of Dr. William Palmer of Rugeley: Together with a Full Account of the Murder of John P. Cook and a Short Account of His Trial in May 1856.* London: T. Fisher Unwin, 1925.

Furner, M. O. *Advocacy & Objectivity: A Crisis in the Professionalization of American Social Science, 1865–1905.* Lexington: University Press of Kentucky, 1975.

Gillin, J. L. "The Personality of Edward Alsworth Ross." *American Journal of Sociology* 42 (1937): 534–42.

Gowers, W. R. *A Manual of Diseases of the Nervous System.* 2 vols. 1886–88. 2d ed. London: J. & A. Churchill, 1892–93.

Hawaii Supreme Court Reports. Vol. 36: 793–95. N.d.

Hawaii Supreme Court Reports. Vol. 43: 430–32. N.d.

Humphris, F. H. "Feasting in Hawaii." *Paradise of the Pacific* 19 (1906): 12.

———. "What Is Pain? An Enquiry into Its Nature and Origin." *Transactions of the Hawaiian Territorial Medical Society,* 1906: 98–109.

———. "What Is Pain? An Attempt to Define Its Origin and Nature." *Journal of Advanced Therapeutics* 26 (1908): 63–78.

———. "Presidential Address Delivered Before the Twenty-Third Annual Meeting of the American Electro-Therapeutic Association." *Journal of Advanced Therapeutics* 31 (1913): 349–55.

———. "On Ascertaining the Depth of Foreign Bodies Simply and Immediately by Screening." *Journal of Advanced Therapeutics* 33 (1915): 40–42.

———. "Melted Paraffin Wax Bath." *American Journal of Electrotherapeutics and Radiology* 37 (1919): 61–64.

———. "Anterior Poliomyelitis." *American Journal of Electrotherapeutics and Radiology* 39 (1921): 458–60.

———. *Artificial Sunlight and Its Therapeutic Uses.* 2d ed. London: H. Milford, Oxford University Press, 1925.

———. "Light in the Prevention of Rickets." *American Journal of Electrotherapeutics and Radiology* 43 (1925): 263–66.

———. "Light and Its Therapeutics: Being the Presidential Address Delivered Before the Hunterian Society in Its One Hundred and Sixth Year." *Physical Therapeutics* 45 (1927): 23–27.

———. "Electricity in the Relief of Pain." *Healing Island,* no. 4. Kamuela, Hawaii: Archaeus Project, 1998.

Isenberg, E. W. *Early Memories and Old Stories.* San Diego: n.p., 1974.

James, William. *The Will to Believe and Other Essays in Popular Philosophy.* New York: Longmans, Green, 1896 [t.p. 1898]. Reprint. New York: Dover Publications, 1956.

———. *Memories and Studies.* New York: Longmans, Green, 1911.

Jordan, David Starr. *Life's Enthusiasms.* Boston: Beacon Press, 1906.

———. *The Heredity of Richard Roe: A Discussion of the Principles of Eugenics.* Boston: American Unitarian Association, 1911.

———. *The Days of a Man,* 2 vols. Yonkers-on-Hudson, N.Y.: World Book Co., 1922.

———. *The Story of a Good Woman: Jane Lathrop Stanford.* Yonkers-on-Hudson, N.Y.: World Book Co., 1922.

Katsuki, Betty. "Medical Men Who Helped to Shape Hawaii." *Hawaii Medical Journal* 40 (1981): 279–82.

Katsuki, Ichitaro. "Suggestion and Suggestibility." *Transactions of the Hawaiian Territorial Medical Society,* 1908: 54–60.

Knott, G. H., ed. *Trial of William Palmer.* London: W. Hodge, 1912.

"Leland Stanford Junior University." *Science,* n.s., 13 (1901): 142–43.

Marberry, M. M. *The Golden Voice: A Biography of Isaac Kalloch.* New York: Farrar, Straus, 1947.

McLaren, Angus. *A Prescription for Murder: The Victorian Serial Killings of Dr. Thomas Neill Cream.* Chicago: University of Chicago Press, 1993.

Metzger, W. P. *Academic Freedom in the Age of the University.* New York: Columbia University Press, 1961.

Mirrielees, E. R. *Stanford: The Story of a University.* New York: G. P. Putnam's Sons, 1959.

Mohr, J. C. "Academic Turmoil and Public Opinion: The Ross Case at Stanford." *Pacific Historical Review* 39 (1970): 39–61.

Moran, H. A. *David Starr Jordan: His Spirit and Decision of Character.* Palo Alto, Calif.: Daily Press, 1969.

Nagel, G. W. *Jane Stanford: Her Life and Letters.* Stanford, Calif.: Stanford Alumni Association, 1975.

———. *Iron Will: The Life and Letters of Jane Stanford.* Rev. ed. Stanford, Calif.: Stanford Alumni Association, 1985.

Nash, G. H. *Herbert Hoover and Stanford University.* Stanford, Calif.: Hoover Institution Press, 1988.

Norris, Frank. *The Octopus.* New York: Doubleday, Page, 1901.

Offord, Lenore G. "'The Gifts of Cordelia': The Case of Cordelia Botkin." In *San Francisco Murders,* ed. J. H. Jackson. New York: Duell, Sloan & Pearce, 1947.

Ogle, Gary. "The Mysterious Death of Mrs. Leland Stanford." *Pacific Historian* 25 (1981): 1–7. Reprint, ed., *Honolulu Advertiser*, July 27, 1981.

Older, C. [Mrs. Fremont]. *San Francisco: Magic City*. New York: Longmans, Green, 1961.

Ophüls, William. *Arteriosclerosis. Cardiovascular Disease: Their Relation to Infectious Diseases*. Stanford, Calif.: Stanford University Press, 1921.

Potter, S. O. L. *A Handbook of Materia Medica, Pharmacy and Therapeutics: Including the Physiological Action of Drugs, the Special Therapeutics of Disease, Official and Practical Pharmacy, and Minute Directions for Prescription Writing*. 9th ed. Philadelphia: P. Blakiston's Son, 1902.

Pratt, J. S. B., Jr. *The Hawaii I Remember*. Honolulu: Tongg Publishing, 1965.

"The Progress of Science." *Popular Science Monthly* 58 (1901): 663–64.

Quarter Centenary Record of the Class of 1898 of the College of Physicians and Surgeons, Columbia University in the City of New York. Quarter Century Reunion. N.p., December 8, 1923.

Queen's Alumni Review. N.p., April 1934.

Report of the Committee of Economists on the Dismissal of Professor Ross from Leland Stanford Junior University. N.p, 1901.

Report of the President of the Board of Health of the Territory of Hawaii for the Six Months Ending June 30, 1905. Honolulu: Bulletin Publishing Co., 1905.

Ross, E. A. "Social Control. XVIII. The Radiant Points of Social Control." *American Journal of Sociology* 6 (1900): 238–47.

———. "Social Control. XIX. Class Control." *American Journal of Sociology* 6 (1900): 381–95.

———. *Seventy Years of It: An Autobiography*. New York: D. Appleton-Century, 1936.

Schreiner, O., and E. C. Shorey. "Chemical Nature of Soil Organic Matter." *United States Bureau of Soils Bulletin*, no. 74. Washington, D.C.: Government Printing Office, 1910.

———. "A Beneficial Organic Constituent of Soils: Creatinine." *United States Bureau of Soils Bulletin*, no. 83. Washington, D.C.: Government Printing Office, 1911.

Shorey, E. C. "The Deterioration of Raw Cane Sugar in Transit or Storage." *Journal of the Society of Chemical Industry* 17 (1898): 555–58.

———. "Lime an Essential Factor in the Forage." *Hawaii Agricultural Experiment Station Press Bulletin*, no. 15 (1906): 1–6.

———. "Organic Nitrogen in Hawaiian Soil." *Hawaii Agricultural Experiment Station Press Bulletin*, no. 20 (1907): 37–59.

———. "The Presence of Some Benzene Derivatives in Soils." *Journal of Agricultural Research* 1 (1914): 357–63.

Shorey, E. C., W. H. Fry, and W. Hazen. "Calcium Compounds in Soils." *Journal of Agricultural Research* 8 (1917): 57–77.

Siddall, J. W., ed. *Men of Hawaii: A Biographical Reference Library, Com-*

plete and Authentic, of the Men of Note and Substantial Achievement in the Hawaiian Islands. Territory of Hawaii: Honolulu Star-Bulletin, 1921.

Simon, H. B., and M. N. Swartz. "Anaerobic Infections." Pt. 7, ch. V in *Scientific American Medicine*, ed. D. C. Dale and D. D. Federman. New York: Scientific American, 1995.

Smith, J. G. "The Function of the Experiment Station." *Hawaii Agricultural Experiment Station Press Bulletin*, no. 1 (1903).

———. "All About the Hawaii Experiment Station." *Hawaii Agricultural Experiment Station Press Bulletin*, no. 18 (1906): 1–14.

Sorkin, L. S., and S. Puig. "Neuronal Model of Tactile Allodynia Produced by Spinal Strychnine. Effects of Excitatory Amino Acid Receptor Antagonists and a μ-Opiate Receptor Agonist." *Pain* 68 (1996): 283–92.

Spoehr, L. W. "'Progress' Pilgrim: David Starr Jordan and the Circle of Reform, 1891–1931." Ph.D. diss., Stanford University, 1975.

Stern, B. J. "The Ward-Ross Correspondence 1891–1896." *American Sociological Review* 3 (1938): 362–401.

———. "The Ward-Ross Correspondence II 1897–1901." *American Sociological Review* 11 (1946): 593–605.

———. "The Ward-Ross Correspondence II 1897–1901." *American Sociological Review* 11 (1946): 734–48.

———. "The Ward-Ross Correspondence III 1902–1903." *American Sociological Review* 12 (1947): 703–20.

Tanner, A. E. *Studies in Spiritism.* New York: Appleton, 1910. Reprint, Buffalo, New York: Prometheus Books, 1994.

Tanner, T. H. *Memoranda on Poisons.* 11th rev. ed. Philadelphia: P. Blakiston's Son, 1912.

Taylor, A. S. *On Poisons in Relation to Medical Jurisprudence and Medicine.* 1848. 3d ed. Philadelphia: H. C. Lea, 1875.

Teilhet H., and A. Boucher. "'The Demon in the Belfry': The Case of Theodore Durrant—1895–." In *San Francisco Murders,* ed. J. H. Jackson. New York: Duell, Sloan & Pearce, 1947.

Three Years After: Triennial Record of the Class of Ninety-four, Princeton University. Philadelphia: John McGill White & Frank Clinton Smythe, N.d.

Transactions of the Fifteenth Annual Meeting of the Hawaiian Territorial Medical Society. Honolulu: Paradise of the Pacific Print, 1907.

Transactions of the Sixteenth Annual Meeting of the Hawaiian Territorial Medical Society. Honolulu: Hawaiian Star Print, 1908.

Transactions of the Seventeenth Annual Meeting of the Hawaiian Territorial Medical Society. Honolulu: Hawaiian Star Print, 1909.

Transactions of the Eighteenth Annual Meeting of the Hawaiian Territorial Medical Society. Honolulu: Hawaiian Gazette Co., 1910.

"The Treatment of Strychnine Poisoning." *Journal of the American Medical Association* 98 (1932): 1992–94.

Tutorow, N. E. *Leland Stanford: Man of Many Careers.* Menlo Park, Calif.: Pacific Coast Publishers, 1971.

Van Dine, D. L. "The Introduction of Top-Minnows into the Hawaiian Islands." *Hawaii Agricultural Research Station Press Bulletin,* no. 20 (1907): 1–10.

Ward, L. F. "Contemporary Sociology. III." *American Journal of Sociology* 7 (1902): 749–62.

Waterhouse, E. C. "Some Observations on a Case of Nephro-Lithiasis." *Transactions of the Hawaiian Territorial Medical Society,* 1906, 59–64.

———. *"Restriction" of Rubber from an American Viewpoint.* Honolulu: Advertiser Publishing Co., 1923.

Wilson, Gretchen. *With All Her Might: The Life of Gertrude Harding Militant Suffragette.* Fredericton, N.B.: Goose Lane Editions, 1996. Reprint. New York: Holmes & Meier, 1998.

Wilson, S. A. K. *Neurology.* 2 vols. Baltimore: Williams & Wilkins, 1940.

Index